The Trail of Tears and Indian Removal

AMY H. STURGIS

Greenwood Guides to Historic Events, 1500–1900
Linda S. Frey and Marsha L. Frey, Series Editors

GREENWOOD PRESS
Westport, Connecticut • London

Library of Congress Cataloging-in-Publication Data

Sturgis, Amy H., 1971–
 The Trail of Tears and Indian removal / Amy H. Sturgis.
 p. cm.—(Greenwood guides to historic events, 1500–1900, ISSN
1538-442X)
 Includes bibliographical references and index.
 ISBN 0-313-33658-X (alk. paper)
 1. Trail of Tears, 1838. 2. Cherokee Indians—Relocation.
3. Cherokee Indians—Government relations. 4. Cherokee Indians—
Social conditions. I. Title.
E99.C5S93   2007
973.04′97557—dc22   2006028658

British Library Cataloguing in Publication Data is available.

Library of Congress Catalog Card Number: 2006028658
ISBN: 0-313-33658-X
ISSN: 1538-442X

First published in 2007

Greenwood Press, 88 Post Road West, Westport, CT 06881
An imprint of Greenwood Publishing Group, Inc.
www.greenwood.com

Printed in the United States of America

The paper used in this book complies with the
Permanent Paper Standard issued by the National
Information Standards Organization (Z39.48–1984).

10 9 8 7 6 5 4 3 2 1

For my parents,
Donald R. and Karen H. Sturgis,
with love and gratitude

CONTENTS

Photographs follow page 82.

SERIES FOREWORD

American statesman Adlai Stevenson stated, "We can chart our future clearly and wisely only when we know the path which has led to the present." This series, Greenwood Guides to Historic Events, 1500–1900, is designed to illuminate that path by focusing on events from 1500 to 1900 that have shaped the world. The years 1500 to 1900 include what historians call the early modern period (1500 to 1789, the onset of the French Revolution) and part of the modern period (1789 to 1900).

In 1500, an acceleration of key trends marked the beginnings of an interdependent world and the posing of seminal questions that changed the nature and terms of intellectual debate. The series closes with 1900, the inauguration of the twentieth century. This period witnessed profound economic, social, political, cultural, religious, and military changes. An industrial and technological revolution transformed the modes of production, marked the transition from a rural to an urban economy, and ultimately raised the standard of living. Social classes and distinctions shifted. The emergence of the territorial and later the national state altered man's relations with and view of political authority. The shattering of the religious unity of the Roman Catholic world in Europe marked the rise of a new pluralism. Military revolutions changed the nature of warfare. The books in this series emphasize the complexity and diversity of the human tapestry and include political, economic, social, intellectual, military, and cultural topics. Some of the authors focus on events in U.S. history such as the Salem witchcraft trials, the American Revolution, the abolitionist movement, and the Civil War. Others analyze European topics, such as the Reformation and Counter-Reformation and the French Revolution. Still others bridge cultures and continents by examining the voyages of discovery, the

Atlantic slave trade, and the Age of Imperialism. Some focus on intellectual questions that have shaped the modern world, such as Charles Darwin's *Origin of Species*, or on turning points such as the Age of Romanticism. Others examine defining economic, religious, or legal events or issues such as the building of the railroads, the Second Great Awakening, and abolitionism. Heroes (e.g., Meriwether Lewis and William Clark), scientists (e.g., Darwin), military leaders (e.g., Napoleon Bonaparte), poets (e.g., Lord Byron) stride across the pages. Many of these events were seminal in that they marked profound changes or turning points. The Scientific Revolution, for example, changed the way individuals viewed themselves and their world.

The authors, acknowledged experts in their fields, synthesize key events, set developments within the larger historical context, and, most important, present well-balanced, well-written accounts that integrate the most recent scholarship in the field.

The topics were chosen by an advisory board composed of historians, high school history teachers, and school librarians to support the curriculum and meet student research needs. The volumes are designed to serve as resources for student research and to provide clearly written interpretations of topics central to the secondary school and lower-level undergraduate history curriculum. Each author outlines a basic chronology to guide the reader through often-confusing events and presents a historical overview to set those events within a narrative framework. Three to five topical chapters underscore critical aspects of the event. In the final chapter the author examines the impact and consequences of the event. Biographical sketches furnish background on the lives and contributions of the players who strut across the stage. Ten to fifteen primary documents, ranging from letters to diary entries, song lyrics, proclamations, and posters, cast light on the event, provide material for student essays, and stimulate critical engagement with the sources. Introductions identify the authors of the documents and the main issues. In some cases a glossary of selected terms is provided as a guide to the reader. Each work contains an annotated bibliography of recommended books, articles, CD-ROMs, Internet sites, videos, and films that set the materials within the historical debate.

Reading these works can lead to a more sophisticated understanding of the events and debates that have shaped the modern world and can stimulate a more active engagement with the issues that still affect us. It has been a particularly enriching experience to work closely with such dedicated professionals. We have come to know and value even more highly the authors in this series and our editors at Greenwood, particularly Kevin Ohe and Michael Hermann. In many cases they have become more than colleagues; they have become friends. To them and to future historians we dedicate this series.

Linda S. Frey
University of Montana

Marsha L. Frey
Kansas State University

PREFACE

The Trail of Tears takes its name from the Cherokee description of the event, which translates as "the trail where they cried." Perhaps no event better captures the mid-nineteenth century shift in U.S. Indian policy, or the cost of the ideology of Manifest Destiny, the belief that it was the God-given right of white U.S. citizens to expand their power across the continent, than the forced removal of the Cherokee Nation from its traditional homeland in 1838–1839.

Traditional introductory accounts of the Trail of Tears often consider the event as it relates to President Andrew Jackson's vision of his nation (and of Native Americans), as a terrible tragedy because of the loss of life that followed from it, but an inevitable product of the growth and maturation of the United States. In fact, the Trail of Tears underscores several paradoxical aspects of Andrew Jackson's legacy. First, in key ways Jackson's administration was a departure from, and not a continuation of, the tradition begun by founders such as Thomas Jefferson. Jackson did not continue the civilization campaign that encouraged American Indians to acculturate and assimilate; in fact, his policies punished the most acculturated and assimilated of the native nations, the so-called "civilized tribes."

Second, Indian removal was not inevitable. Had the U.S. political system functioned as it was meant to function—that is, if the executive had enforced the decision of the judiciary in the case of *Worcester v. Georgia*, and if Congress had refused to ratify an illegal treaty in the case of the Treaty of New Echota—the Trail of Tears might not have happened—at least, not in the manner that it did. Third, the "Jacksonian revolution" gave rise to a number of reform movements. Many of the leaders of such groups were the first to denounce the removal policy as unjust and inhumane. The products of Jacksonianism, in effect, opposed the policies of Jacksonianism.

This volume provides an intellectual history of the ideas and policies that made the Trail of Tears possible. One of the key components of the story is the internal struggle of the Cherokee Nation as its culture and political structure changed in response to contact with the United States. The Cherokee literacy revolution underscored the factions within the Cherokee Nation—those who sought assimilation with the United States, those who sought to adopt certain practices, such as Christianity, while remaining a separate people, and those who wished to separate and maintain a more traditional way of life. Leaders of these groups came into conflict when faced with the threat of removal, and their various choices to trust the U.S. system, to appease its representatives, to fight, to flee, and to assume responsibility for implementing policies they had opposed, had tremendous implications for the experience of removal.

The Trail of Tears left the Cherokees not only with thousands dead, but also with a nation geographically divided, and those in so-called Indian Territory suffering dramatic internal political and cultural schisms. If the Trail of Tears is significant in the history of the United States, it had far more impact on the history of the Cherokee Nation, and this volume reflects the tremendous influence that forced removal had on the Cherokee people and their nation.

By studying the Cherokee as well as the U.S. side of the Trail of Tears, a full picture emerges of a turning point in U.S. American Indian policy. By asking how this tragedy could have happened, we may discover ways to avoid repeating such events in the future.

ACKNOWLEDGMENTS

My thanks go to Michael Hermann for inviting me to participate in this series, Mariah Gumpert for guiding this project, and Marsha L. Frey for her helpful comments.

As parts of this text reflect work first undertaken on behalf of my dissertation while a graduate student at Vanderbilt University, I wish to thank Paul K. Conkin, my advisor, and Thomas A. Schwartz, my committee chair, as well as Joyce E. Chaplin and Beth Ann Conklin for their assistance. I likewise thank Lewis Perry, Margo Todd, and the late Hugh Davis Graham for their encouragement and guidance.

I also owe a debt of gratitude to the Belmont University students in my Spring 2006 liberal studies course on the Trail of Tears, including Tiffany Cagle, Charles Harper, Erica Johnson, Laura Kittleson, Irene Ma, Emily Pope, Brooke Robinson, and Mark Rucker, as well as Grace Walker Monk.

I am grateful to the staffs of the Belmont University and Vanderbilt University libraries for their assistance. I thank my parents, grandparents, and sister for their support. The Shire's Virginia Lórien has my gratitude for her enthusiastic editorial involvement. Most importantly, I thank my dear husband, Larry M. Hall, to whom I owe more than I can ever repay. Any errors remaining in this work are my own.

CHRONOLOGY OF EVENTS

1785   The Treaty of Hopewell becomes the first treaty between the United States and the Cherokee Nation. This agreement establishes recognized borders between the two nations, and makes U.S. citizens within Cherokee territory subject to Cherokee law.

1788   The U.S. Constitution is ratified.

1789   George Washington is inaugurated president of the United States.

1791   The Treaty of Holston pledges "perpetual peace between the United States and the Cherokee Nation." This treaty institutes the U.S. "civilization program" among the Cherokees, officially recognizes the borders of the Cherokee Nation, notes the jurisdiction of the U.S. courts for crimes committed outside of Cherokee lands and the Cherokee courts for crimes committed on Cherokee lands, and gives the United States exclusive rights in regulating trade with the Cherokee Nation.

1796   President George Washington begins the "civilization program" among the Cherokees.

1796   John Adams is elected president of the United States.

1800   Moravians establish a mission for the Cherokees.

1800   Thomas Jefferson is elected president of the United States.

1802   The United States and Georgia agree to the Compact of 1802 regarding ownership of future ceded American Indian lands.

1806–1809	Shawnee warrior Tecumseh, along with his brother Tenskwatawa, or The Prophet, travel the United States. Together they offer a message of pan-Indian unity, calling for spiritual renewal and military resistance against the U.S. forces seeking to take and control Native American lands. Tecumseh emerges as the most influential American Indian political leader in the United States.
1808	James Madison is elected president of the United States.
1808–1810	Cherokees move west of the Mississippi River in the first voluntary mass migration from Cherokee lands.
1809	Hillis Hayo (or Josiah Francis), leader of the Creeks, the most powerful of the Southern native nations, invites Tecumseh to visit Florida and Louisiana. The two become allies, thus strengthening Tecumseh's movement.
1809	The Treaty of Fort Wayne, Indiana, sets the precedent for the United States to recognize illegitimate documents as official treaties. In this case, the agreement providing for the sale of Shawnee lands was signed not by Shawnee officials, but instead by a group of Potawatomi leaders known by some as the "whiskey chiefs," who signed away the rights to lands they did not own.
1811	The Battle of Tippecanoe, in which William Henry Harrison's troops attacked the growing American Indian alliance in Florida, ends with a U.S. victory. Harrison forces the Shawnees and their allies into ceding large amounts of land; his success eventually propels him to the presidency.
1812	Creek civil war erupts in Georgia and Florida between the Upper Creeks, or Red Sticks, who wish to resist U.S. interference and encroachment, and the Lower Creeks, who favor land cession and Christianization.
1812–1815	The War of 1812 is fought between the United States and Great Britain, with American Indians allied on both sides.
1813	Tecumseh dies while fighting against the United States during the War of 1812.
1813	The Upper Creeks (Red Sticks) attack U.S. citizens at Fort Mims in southern Alabama, killing more than 350.

Cherokees, including John Ross and Major Ridge, fight on the side of the United States and the Lower Creeks against the Red Sticks.

1813   Although the Seminole villages in northern Florida technically are in Spanish territory, not on U.S. land, the Tennessee militia raids these areas. One of the militia leaders is Andrew Jackson.

1814   Andrew Jackson leads 5,000 troops to retaliate against the Creeks for the attack on Fort Mims. At the Battle of Horseshoe Bend, Jackson's forces kill more than 1,000 Creek men, women, and children. Jackson then forces not only the Upper Creeks, who had attacked Fort Mims, but also the Lower Creeks, who had allied with the United States and assisted Jackson's campaign, to cede more than 20 million acres of Creek land to the U.S. government. Jackson secures his reputation as an "Indian fighter."

1815   Jackson's victory at the Battle of New Orleans, accomplished with the help of Choctaw allies, begins to build the momentum for his bid for the presidency.

1816   James Monroe is elected president of the United States.

1817   Some Cherokee leaders, including Sequoyah, cede lands in Georgia for lands in Arkansas (in areas that would become Oklahoma). Several thousand Cherokees begin to emigrate west because of harassment from white settlers, particularly in Georgia. The remaining Cherokees adopt articles of government giving only the National Council the right to cede additional Cherokee lands. American Board of Commissioners for Foreign Missions and Baptist missionaries arrive among the Cherokees.

1817–1818   Andrew Jackson leads U.S. forces against the Seminoles on the border of Georgia and Florida in order to remove the Seminoles and force the Spanish to give Florida to the United States. During this First Seminole War, Jackson tricks Creek leader Hillis Hayo (Josiah Francis) into boarding a U.S. gunboat by flying the flag of Great Britain, ally to the Creeks. Jackson executes him.

1819 The Cherokee National Council cedes additional land east of the Mississippi River in exchange for lands in the west. Some North Carolina Cherokees accept reservation lands outside of Cherokee Nation borders.

1821 Sequoyah, or George Gist, develops a syllabary to allow the Cherokee tongue to become a written language.

1822 The Cherokee Nation creates a Supreme Court.

1824 John Quincy Adams is elected president of the United States.

1825 The Seminoles, under the leadership of Osceola, continue the war. The United States claims the rights to all Seminole lands east of the Mississippi River.

1825 Although the Creek Nation had voted that ceding Creek Nation land to the U.S. government was a capital crime, Chief William MacIntosh accepts $25,000 to sign a document ceding all Creek lands in Georgia and much in Alabama. MacIntosh is killed by fellow Creeks for his actions. President John Quincy Adams rejects the treaty as illegitimate, but negotiates another allowing the United States to retain some Creek lands.

1827 Pathkiller, the principal chief of the Cherokee Nation responsible for plans to reorganize the Cherokee Nation so it might better negotiate with and resist the United States, dies, as does his successor, Charles Hicks. The Constitution of the Cherokee Nation, modeled after the U.S. Constitution, is ratified.

1828 Pathkiller's secretary, John Ross, is elected principal chief of the Cherokee Nation. In New Echota he builds a national capital with buildings devoted to the different branches of the Cherokee government. *The Cherokee Phoenix*, a bilingual Cherokee newspaper, begins publication with Elias Boudinot as its editor. Andrew Jackson is elected president of the United States.

1828–1829 The state of Georgia extends its legal jurisdiction to Cherokee Nation lands and nullifies Cherokee law. The Georgia legislature passes laws making it illegal for

Cherokees to mine gold on their own land, testify against whites in court, or have political assemblies.

1829   Gold is discovered on Cherokee land. White settlers violate Cherokee borders to search for gold. Principal Chief John Ross protests in Washington, D.C., about Georgia's aggressions against the Cherokee Nation. Andrew Jackson articulates his removal policy, and Jeremiah Evarts publishes his "William Penn" essays reflecting popular outrage at this plan.

1831   The U.S. Supreme Court calls the Cherokee Nation a "domestic dependent nation" in *Cherokee Nation v. Georgia*.

1832   The U.S. Supreme Court upholds the Cherokee Nation's sovereignty against the state of Georgia in *Worcester v. Georgia*.

1835   Leaders of the Cherokee Treaty Party such as Elias Boudinot, Major Ridge, and John Ridge, without legitimate authority, negotiate and sign the Treaty of New Echota, which cedes Cherokee lands in the East to the United States in return for payment and assistance with removal to Indian Territory. Cherokees are given two years to evacuate their lands.

1836   The U.S. Senate ratifies the Treaty of New Echota by one vote, despite vocal protest from the Cherokee Nation. Martin Van Buren is elected president of the United States.

1838–1839 U.S. forces under the command of General Winfield Scott begin rounding up Cherokees on May 23, 1838. The Trail of Tears begins with Cherokees held in military stockades and then moved in multiple contingents over land and water. Between deaths in the internment camps, en route, and upon arrival in Indian Territory, the Cherokee death toll rises to 25–35 percent of those forced to leave their lands. Removal takes ten months. Tsali, one of a small band of Cherokees who eluded capture, surrenders to the U.S. forces who seek him, and in return the remaining Cherokees are left in the North Carolina mountains.

CHAPTER 1

OVERVIEW: THE TRAIL OF TEARS AS TURNING POINT

Visitors who travel to Cherokee, North Carolina, today have the opportunity to attend what has been called "America's most popular outdoor drama," the play *Unto These Hills*.[1] The Mountainside Theater, home to *Unto These Hills*, estimates that more than five million people have watched the seasonal performance since its debut on July 1, 1950. Led by performers of Cherokee descent, the show tells the story of the Cherokee Nation from contact with Hernando de Soto in 1540 until the advent of forced removal by the U.S. government in 1838.

For the complete story of removal, one must travel to Tahlequah, Oklahoma, the capital of the Cherokee Nation of Oklahoma. There at the Tsa La Gi ("Cherokee") Amphitheater at the Cherokee Heritage Center, a different outdoor drama is performed, entitled *The Trail of Tears*. In stark contrast to this story of the coerced relocation of the Cherokees in 1838–1839, the Cherokee Cultural Center also offers guests the opportunity to explore the Ancient Village, a living history exhibit that depicts Cherokee life prior to European contact. Since 1967, the Ancient Village has provided educational tours allowing visitors to observe a day in the life of a pre-Contact Cherokee community and gain a sense of Cherokee social history and cultural practices. The clothing, props, and setting of the village are authentic: only one ingredient is left to the visitor's imagination. One must picture the portrayed events taking place not in present-day Oklahoma, but in the historic Cherokee territory, eight hundred miles to the east. The *Trail of Tears* drama offers an explanation of why the Ancient Village was not built in the traditional Cherokee homeland.

The road from Cherokee, North Carolina, to Tahlequah, Oklahoma, is dotted with official markers denoting the routes known collectively as the historic Trail of Tears. As it winds through Middle Tennessee, it passes by another historic site known as the Hermitage, the family home of President Andrew Jackson. The stately manor, with its tree-lined drive and garden walks, seems far removed from the suffering and death portrayed in the *Trail of Tears* drama, but it is as central to the removal story as the trail routes themselves. Visitors are left to reconcile the domestic tranquility and civilized peace represented by the Hermitage with the nearby evidence of its owner's legacy.

No ancient village or preserved home provides a tangible marker to bring a third piece of the Trail of Tears puzzle to attention. A third party, however, was involved with the story as well. African and African American slaves were owned not only by the white U.S. citizens who enforced removal, but also by some of the Cherokees who were its victims.

Named after the Cherokee designation, which translates as "the trail where they cried," the Trail of Tears is the name commonly given to the forced removal of the Cherokee Nation from its lands by the United States, and the relocation of the Cherokee people across the Mississippi River to so-called "Indian Territory," an area in the present-day state of Oklahoma. Not only did the Cherokees lose their ancestral home during this 1838–1839 campaign, but many also lost their lives. Traditional estimates suggest more than 4,000 of 15,000 Cherokees died during or as a result of removal; some recent recalculations suggest a higher death toll of approximately 8,000 out of 21,500.[2]

At the end of the day, the contemporary student of history is left with a series of baffling and disturbing questions when considering the Trail of Tears. Who was at fault? Why did it happen? How could it have been prevented? How can similar events be avoided in the future? The answers to these questions, when answers do exist, are complex. The importance of asking them, however, cannot be overstated. The most fruitful avenue of inquiry into the Trail of Tears is the consideration of the political, social, and legal ideas— U.S. as well as Cherokee—motivating the key figures involved in the event.

Such a pursuit is most certainly worthwhile. The story of the Trail of Tears continues to command attention and remain relevant because, from a variety of perspectives, it represents a turning point in history.

For the World

Viewed as an event on the stage of world history, the Trail of Tears supplies one example of the international, ongoing phenomenon of ethnic cleansing. In 1994, a United Nations Commission of Experts defined ethnic cleansing in the following manner:

> Ethnic cleansing is a purposeful policy designed by one ethnic or religious group to remove by violent and terror-inspiring means the civilian population of another ethnic or religious group from certain geographical areas. To a large extent, it is carried out in the name of misguided nationalism, historic grievances, and a powerful driving sense of revenge. This purpose appears to be the occupation of territory to the exclusion of the purged group or groups.[3]

If applied retroactively to the removal of the Cherokee Nation in 1838–1839, the 1994 definition fits. Certainly the policy was purposeful. Far from being a sudden, spontaneous whim of the U.S. government, the policy of removal required long-term logistical planning—the purchase of new federal boats, the mustering of seven thousand troops, and the readying of multiple "collection camps" to hold detainees, for example. Though soldiers utilized the element of surprise when they captured the Cherokee citizens, the action itself was not altogether unexpected. Removal loomed on the horizon first when the Indian Removal Act of 1830 was passed by the Twenty-First Congress of the United States, and then again when President Andrew Jackson indicated he would not execute the U.S. Supreme Court's decision in *Worcester v. Georgia* in 1832, in effect refusing to recognize or protect the Cherokee Nation's territorial rights against the state of Georgia. Removal became inevitable when the U.S. Senate, by one single vote, ratified the New Echota Treaty in 1836, even though no official representative of the Cherokee national government had signed it. The treaty provided two years for voluntary migration, thus giving the U.S. government an excuse to move against the Cherokees in 1838.

The Cherokees as a whole represented more of a separate ethnic group than a separate religious one when contrasted with the white U.S. mainstream. As Cherokee Principal Chief John Ross, *Cherokee Phoenix* editor and Treaty Party leader Elias Boudinot, and numerous others (see "Petition of Cherokee Women" in the Primary Documents) repeatedly pointed out, many Cherokees by that time were Christian, just like their white counterparts in the United States. Much of the rhetoric surrounding and supporting removal was couched in racial terms. Andrew Jackson's response to the Removal Act refers to the "savages," "red men," and "children of the forest."[4] The first pro-removal essay to circulate in the popular press, 1830's "Removal of the Indians" by Michigan Territorial Governor Lewis Cass, put it more plainly, setting up the issue as a clash between "the two races of men, who yet divide this portion of the continent between them." Moreover, Cass exemplified the ease with which many assigned broad, undesirable attributes to all within an ethnic group, asserting that all of the American Indians were by "inherent" nature "less provident in arrangement, less frugal in enjoyment, less industrious in acquiring, more implacable in their resentments, more ungovernable in their passions, with fewer principles to guide them, and with less knowledge to improve and instruct them."[5]

The means of removal were violent, as the death toll clearly indicates. Accounts of spouses separated from each other, and children divided from their parents, underscore the terror of the roundup; removal itself brought the additional horrors of starvation, exposure, and illness. By what terms were such experiences justified? One of the most potent was nationalism, a sense that it was the Manifest Destiny of the United States to expand, conquer, and remake the continent according to its will. With regard to the Native Americans, Jackson claimed removal was part of this process, a necessary step in the nation's evolution: "the present policy of the Government is but a continuation of the same progressive change. . . . The waves of population and civilization are rolling to the westward."[6] Grievances and revenge may have played important, albeit lesser, parts; when General Winfield Scott assumed command of the removal campaign, he felt obliged to remain with the Georgian troops personally, fearing from what he observed that some might choose to execute rather than relocate their prisoners. The Trail of Tears meets the last criteria for ethnic cleansing, the issue of territorial control, most clearly. The overt and obvious goal of removal was to transfer ownership of the land previously held by the Cherokee Nation into the hands of white U.S. citizens.

As a global phenomenon, ethnic cleansing has a history that expands back for centuries if not millennia, and stretches forward to the present day. As historian John Mack Faragher has proved, the Trail of Tears was not the first ethnic cleansing in North America: that distinction appears to belong to the 1755 expulsion of the French Acadians from Nova Scotia by the British government.[7] For that matter, it was not even the first relocation project undertaken by the United States, as the Choctaw, Chickasaw, and Creek Nations all faced removal immediately prior to the Cherokee Nation; although technically these parties agreed to their departure, their decisions were made under extreme duress. The Trail of Tears was, however, the most ambitious political and military campaign of its kind planned and carried out by the U.S. government. It would not be the last. More than once the United States returned to forced removal as national policy, as the Long Walk of the Navajo Nation in 1863–1864 illustrates. More recent events, such as the internment of Japanese Americans during World War II, bear more than a passing resemblance to this pattern.

For the United States

The Trail of Tears was a watershed national event for the United States in two key ways. First, removal signaled a radical departure from previous U.S. policy toward American Indians. Since the first administration of President George Washington, the primary position of the United States toward Native America was defined by the so-called "Indian Civilization" campaign, which encouraged cultural, economic, and political assimilation, and fostered Christianization, agriculture, trade, education, and adoption of European institutions in native nations. Perhaps the most vocal and vehement champion of the program, Washington's Secretary of State and later U.S. President Thomas Jefferson, conceived of it as a "great reformation."[8] A series of laws governing "Trade and Intercourse with the Indians" opened with the first act in 1790 and included amendments and renewals in 1793, 1796, 1802, and 1822.

As part of this plan, the United States recognized the American Indians as the owners of the land on which they lived, with the rights to cede or sell these lands as well as to retain them. As Jefferson explained to native leaders, "We, indeed, are always ready to buy land; but we will never ask but when you wish to sell...."[9] When queried about this by a British minister in 1792, Jefferson clarified: "We consider it as established by the usage of different nations into a kind of *Jus gentium* for America, that a white nation settling down and declaring that such and such are their limits, makes an invasion of those limits by any other white nation an act of war, but gives no right of soil against the native possessors."[10]

Jefferson's first introduction to the Cherokees came in the impressive form of the Cherokee chief and orator Ostenaco. Jefferson's father frequently entertained Ostenaco when he came to Williamsburg, and young Jefferson knew him as a distinguished guest in the family's home at Shadwell. In 1762 Jefferson also saw Ostenaco deliver an address at the university Jefferson attended, William and Mary College, before the Cherokee leader set sail for London to visit King George III. It is not a leap to imagine Jefferson revisiting such memories when assessing the feasibility of a joined future between all whites and American Indians: "You will unite yourselves with us, join in our great councils and form one people with us, and we shall all be Americans; you will mix with us by marriage, your blood will run in our veins, and will spread with us over this great island."[11]

If anything, Jefferson's perspective on Native America was the product of his idealization of indigenous Americans, using them to symbolize the noble savage in what he imagined as a pre-government state of nature. He wrote in 1787: "And we think ours a bad government. The only condition on earth to be compared to ours, in my opinion, is that of the Indian, where they have still less law than we. The European, are governments of kites over pigeons."[12] As a rhetorical device the archetypal Indian served the purposes of Jefferson's political theory. To be fair, Jefferson tended to reduce the Europeans to equally abstract symbols, as well: "I am convinced that those societies (as the Indians) which live without government, enjoy in their general mass an infinitely greater degree of happiness than those who live under the European governments. Among the former, public opinion is in the place of law, and restrains morals as powerfully as laws ever did anywhere. Among the latter, under pretense of governing, they have divided into two classes, the wolves and sheep."[13] When contrasted with European "wolves" and "sheep," in fact, the American Indians appeared in a good light indeed.

Forced removal not only marked an abandonment of the civilization campaign and the legal promises made to Native Americans about their property rights, then, but it also reflected a different view of American Indians. Rather than potential siblings in the body politic to be embraced and enfolded, if often remodeled after a European ideal along the way, the Native Americans were savages, even subhumans, in the eyes of removal-era leaders. Perhaps this is no surprise in a period in which presidents such as Andrew Jackson and William Henry Harrison used their fame as "Indian fighters" to pave their respective roads to the White House. To such men, native groups such as the Cherokee Nation represented the Other in a distinctly different way than they did to earlier founders such as Washington and Jefferson.

The Trail of Tears marked a somewhat uneasy transition in U.S. political thought from Jeffersonianism to Jacksonianism. Thomas Jefferson's dreams for his fledgling country rested on an ideal: the yeoman farmer. Such a man embodied the ideas to which Jefferson was most committed. With his hands in the soil he owned and improved, the yeoman farmer was independent and self-sufficient, tied to the land that provided him with food, clothing, and shelter. Owning and working his property gave the yeoman farmer a vested self-interest in the new U.S. experiment, gifting him with a natural inclination toward egalitarianism and an equally natural distrust of authority. In theory, his ability to provide for himself and his family made him jealous of his rights, an unceasing watchdog ever vigilant against powers that might impose authority unjustly or expand power at the expense of individual liberty, even or especially if such forces were the state or national government. Jefferson imagined this hypothetical farmer to be the citizen best equipped to ensure that the republic would endure, a limited state based on checks and balances, strong enough to protect the rights of its citizens, but not so strong that it might expand to become a self-perpetuating tyranny.

Jefferson's view had its contradictions, not the least of which was the conflict between his value of individual freedom and his toleration of the institution of slavery. Moreover, Jefferson's theory underscored an agrarian ideal that, even by the time of the U.S. founding, presented an incomplete picture of economic life, overlooking the commercial and industrial realities of the Northeast and the more urban areas of the South. Furthermore, the pursuit of this ideal required land, and the need for additional land led Jefferson to follow policies with which he himself was at times uncomfortable— for example, the purchase of the Louisiana Territory in the absence of enumerated constitutional powers allowing him to do so. (Incidentally, the Louisiana Territory also provided a place where those American Indians who would not assimilate could retire from white influence and live separately, Jefferson believed. Removal was not altogether absent in his mind, despite his rhetoric.) In other words, Jefferson at times risked expanding the very government he wished to limit, in order to provide additional lands to support more yeoman farmers who would protest actions such as those he just had taken. To his credit, however, he often recognized and wrestled with such moments when pragmatism and ideals collided.

In a way, Jacksonianism was the inevitable if unruly child of Jeffersonianism. Many of the tenets of Jeffersonian thought, such as strict construction of the Constitution and *laissez-faire* economics, provided the backbone of Jacksonianism. As the first president partially elected by the common citizenry—the 1824 election was the first in which free white men without property could vote—Jackson supported expanded suffrage. Also added to this mix was Jackson's loyalty to a potent form of Manifest Destiny, the conviction that the United States possessed a God-given right to expand and control the continent from the Atlantic to the Pacific. His own record as a war hero and Indian fighter added an aggressive, combative flavor to this per-spective. Jefferson's reasoned anti-authoritarianism came from the intellect, and from a comfortable, established home in one of the oldest colonies-turned-states. Jackson's impassioned anti-authoritarianism came from the heart, and from the rugged frontier, where he wielded a horsewhip against man and animal alike with as much practice as his law books, and held all privilege under suspicion. Jefferson responded to opponents with letters and essays; Jackson challenged opponents to duels to the death. Nevertheless, both celebrated—in rhetoric, at least—the farmer, the common man, as the ideal citizen of the United States.

But Jackson's less sophisticated and more personal approach to leadership brought with it extreme paradoxes. He attacked and van-quished the National Bank as a gross overexpansion of the federal government's powers, and then cheerfully ignored the constitutional checks and balances of the system when refusing to enforce the U.S. Supreme Court's decision in *Worcester v. Georgia*. He assaulted the politics of established advantaged and insider networks, yet he insti-tuted the spoils system of patronage, rewarding loyalty in his own supporters and friends rather than merit wherever it could be found. Though he claimed to be democratic, he also insisted that he per-sonified the people and embodied their will (much as Louis XIV asserted that he was France), earning him the nickname "King Andrew I." Under Jackson, the imperial presidency was born, reshap-ing the structure of the federal government and concentrating power in the executive branch. Moreover, the egalitarian movements that sprang up under his leadership, such as those for the abolition of slavery and the rights of women, had little to do with Jackson per-sonally, who was both an unrepentant slaveowner and an adherent of what was, even for its time, a rather eccentric and outmoded under-standing of masculinity (hence his lifelong propensity toward duels, especially when devoted to feminine honor, even after the practice was generally abandoned).

The Trail of Tears brought these contradictions into high relief, as leaders of "Jacksonian" movements such as Catherine Beecher and Ralph Waldo Emerson—pioneers who championed individual rights and condemned unjust and unaccountable use of force—rose up and bitterly protested Jackson's own policy of removal. The children of the Jacksonian movement, it seemed, were disappointed with their father. The history of the United States would continue to stray from Jefferson's attempted, although not always realized, ideals to model Jackson's example, as the political became increasingly personal, and power centralized in the executive branch. It would take decades for abolition, women's suffrage, and other fruits of various Jacksonian movements to be realized—decades too long for words of protest to be of help to the Cherokee Nation.

For the Cherokee Nation

The Trail of Tears, and the related removals of the Choctaws, Creeks, Chickasaws, and others, reflected a change in U.S. policy toward Native America that would yield war and bloodshed for decades to come. The Trail of Tears was one of the first and most dramatic examples of the dispossessing of the American Indians in the nineteenth century, a campaign that eventually visited the Great Plains, Northwest, and Southwest, and affected all Native Americans in the United States.

Obviously the Trail of Tears marked a turning point for the Cherokee Nation, as it meant the loss of Cherokee lands and many Cherokee lives, and the challenge of creating a new existence in Indian Territory. But removal also meant political upheaval for the Cherokees, as violent change underscored the conflicts between pre-existing factions and ripped apart previous loyalties. This followed what already had been a period of rapid transition and transformation for the Cherokees.

When Principal Chief John Ross, the elected executive of the Cherokee Nation, wrote to the U.S. Senate and House of Representatives in 1829, he recounted the recent relations between the Cherokee Nation and the U.S. federal government:

> The great [President] Washington advised a plan and afforded aid for the general improvement of our nation, in agriculture, science, and government. President Jefferson followed the noble example, and concluded an address to our delegation, in language as follows: "I sincerely wish you may succeed in your laudable endeavors to save the remnant of your nation by adopting industrious occupations and a Government of regular law. In thus you may always rely on the counsel and assistance of the United States." This kind and generous policy to meliorate our condition, has been blessed with the happiest results: our

improvement has been without parallel in the history of Indian nations.[14]

Ross's allusion to Cherokee "improvement" referred to the Cherokee response to the Indian civilization program in general, and Thomas Jefferson in particular. Before the campaign, the Cherokees had weighed Cherokee practices against colonial/U.S. ones and accommodated settlers' ways when they had seemed familiar and beneficial, following an age-old pattern of Cherokee adaptability. Cherokee Beloved Woman Nancy Ward, slaveowner, peacemaker, and friend of the whites, embodied the values of the assimilationist Cherokees. But others fought against the idea of becoming like the white settlers and, like leader Dragging Canoe, visibly and violently rebelled. Despite the fact that these Cherokees appeared to represent a minority of the nation, their presence proved that the outcome of the Cherokee/European clash of civilizations had not been decided completely in Cherokee minds.

By the time of the ratification of the U.S. Constitution, many Cherokees had made significant strides in English literacy, established a vibrant trade and agricultural economy, embraced Western agricultural systems including plantation slavery, and called for greater protection of their private property. Jefferson spoke with the Cherokees directly, acknowledging that their progress "has been like grain sown in good ground, producing abundantly," honoring their accomplishments.[15] Jefferson's campaign brought the promise of complete acceptance. If the Cherokees continued to adopt white ways, then they could expect to be welcomed as equals to the citizens of the United States, co-mingling with the members of the other nation.

The Cherokee Nation as a whole seemed to accept this vision of the future. In 1794, the nation unified beneath one principal chief and one second principal chief. With help from the United States the Cherokees created a mounted police force, and by 1808 it protected the entire nation funded solely by Cherokee national money. Statutes in 1809 and 1810 further centralized the Cherokee government by granting greater authority to the elected national council. The Cherokees even assented to eliminating clan revenge for murder, a shift away not only from ancestral homicide law but also from the matrilineal clan system that dispensed it. Soon a literacy revolution, codified law, bilingual presses, and a ratified constitution followed. According to historians such as Mary Young, the Cherokee Nation became a reflection of the United States, a "mirror of the republic"— in this case a very Jeffersonian republic easily recognizable to U.S.

citizens.[16] To many, the Cherokee ideal came to look much like Jefferson's beloved yeoman farmer.

Cherokee leaders referred to the agreement inherent in the civilization campaign often in subsequent years among themselves, and they also used it against U.S. presidents who did not feel bound by its promises of acceptance and respect. For example, Cherokee editor Elias Boudinot reminded the Jackson administration of those that had preceded it:

> It appears now from the communication of the Secretary of War to the Cherokee Delegation, that the illustrious Washington, Jefferson, Madison and Monroe were only tantalizing us, when they encouraged us in pursuit of agriculture and Government, and when they afforded us the protection of the United States, by which we have been preserved to this present time as a nation. . . .[17]

With the dissolution of the civilization campaign came a resurgence of the factionalism that had never disappeared from the Cherokee Nation. Tensions rose between those who had embraced assimilation with U.S. culture and those who had separated, advocating fidelity to traditional Cherokee ways. Some separatists chose to move voluntarily in order to put additional space between the United States and themselves. Among those who remained in the traditional Cherokee lands, further divisions arose between those who maintained faith in the U.S. system and wished to fight removal using its procedures, those who thought yielding to the pressure to relocate was the only means of preserving the lives of Cherokee citizens, and those who simply planned to fight or evade capture when the inevitable occurred.

Certainly many influences affected the internal dynamics of the Cherokee Nation: property holdings, political aspirations, kin loyalties. But the dramatic factionalism of the Cherokee Nation in the 1830s also can be seen as the clash between two specific visions of the Cherokees' future. By 1832, two of the leading voices in the Cherokee Nation—Principal Chief John Ross and *Cherokee Phoenix* editor Elias Boudinot—championed opposing visions of what the Cherokees had accomplished and what they could become. The removal crisis triggered an internal showdown between the former allies, one with drastic and bloody consequences for the entire Cherokee Nation.

In the final analysis, the events surrounding the Trail of Tears set some of the greatest minds of the Cherokee Nation against one another with devastating consequences. Removal ultimately sundered the Cherokees, splitting those many removed west of the Mississippi River from those few who eluded capture, becoming the Eastern Band. Arrival in Indian Territory led to the unification of the newcomers with the Western Cherokees, but also set the stage for Cherokee civil war.

Notes

1. http://www.untothesehills.com (accessed January 10, 2006).

2. Russell Thornton, "The Demography of the Trail of Tears Period: A New Estimate of Cherokee Population Losses," in *Cherokee Removal: Before And After*, ed. William J. Anderson (Athens: University of Georgia Press, 1991), pp. 92–93.

3. *United Nations Commission of Experts' Final Report (S/1994/674)*, Section III.B, available at http://www.ess.uwe.ac.uk/comexpert/III-IV_D.htm#III.B (accessed January 10, 2006).

4. See the Primary Documents section.

5. Lewis Cass, "Removal of the Indians," quoted in *The Cherokee Removal: A Brief History with Documents*, ed. Theda Perdue and Michael D. Green, 2nd ed. (New York: Bedford/St. Martin's, 2005), pp. 115–121, 117, 118.

6. See the Primary Documents section.

7. John Mack Faragher, *A Great and Noble Scheme: The Tragic Story of the Expulsion of the French Acadians from Their American Homeland* (New York: W. W. Norton, 2005).

8. Thomas Jefferson, "To Brother Handsome Lake," November 3, 1802, available at http://libertyonline.hypermall.com/Jefferson/Indian.html (accessed November 9, 2005).

9. Ibid.

10. Jefferson, quoted in Francis Paul Prucha, *The Great Father: The United States Government and the American Indians* (Lincoln: University of Nebraska Press, 1986), p. 22.

11. Jefferson to Captain Henrick, the Delawares, Mohiccans, and Munries, 1808(?), in *The Complete Jefferson*, ed. Saul K. Padover (New York: Duell, Sloan, and Pearce, 1943), pp. 106–107, 106.

12. Jefferson to Rutledge, 1787, in *Thomas Jefferson on Democracy*, ed. Saul K. Padover (New York: Mentor, 1939), p. 25.

13. See Jefferson to Carrington, 1787, in *The Complete Jefferson*, pp. 92–93, 93.

14. The emphases belong to Ross. John Ross to the U.S. Senate and House of Representatives, February 27, 1829, in *The Papers of Chief John Ross*, vol. 1, ed. Gary E. Moulton (Norman: University of Oklahoma Press, 1985), p. 155.

15. "To the Chiefs of the Cherokee Nation," January 10, 1806, in *The Complete Jefferson*, pp. 478–480, 478.

16. Mary Young, "The Cherokee Nation: Mirror of the Republic," *American Quarterly*, no. 33 (Winter 1980): 502–524.

17. Elias Boudinot, June 17, 1829, in *Cherokee Editor: The Writings of Elias Boudinot*, ed. Theda Purdue (Athens: University of Georgia Press, 1996), pp. 108–109, 108.

CHAPTER 2

THE CHEROKEE NATION AND THE LITERACY REVOLUTION

The Cherokee syllabary was designed by an illiterate hermit and perfected by a six-year-old girl in an unremarkable Arkansas cabin. Together, the father-daughter team of Sequoyah and Ahyokeh gave the Cherokees their written language in 1821. Some assimilationist Cherokees, such as Principal Chief John Ross, appreciated Sequoyah's invention in the abstract, as an intellectual feat, but did not learn its symbols. Despite this minority, fluency in the syllabary system spread throughout the nation like wildfire, effectively making Cherokee a literate, rather than simply oral, language virtually overnight. Only Cherokees such as editor Elias Boudinot, however, fully mined the implications of the linguistic shift. In the hands of such men, the syllabary became the spark igniting a burgeoning Cherokee nationalism, and the cornerstone supporting a new concept of Cherokee civilization.

Scholarly debate focuses on the origin of Sequoyah's syllabary and its adoption. Some argue that the syllabary represented an imposed, not indigenous, shift to literacy. Others insist that the Sequoyan revolution was a purely Cherokee affair. Both sides of this imposed/indigenous dichotomy oversimplify the issue. Terms such as "indigenous" and "imposed" become meaningless when we confront the complex and diverse positions of influential Cherokees at the time of the syllabary's invention and acceptance. On the question of assimilation with Western culture, Cherokees such as John Ross, Elias Boudinot, and Sequoyah had radically different positions, dictated by a combination of Cherokee and Western influences.

No Cherokee in the 1820s was purely native, untouched by colonial and U.S. culture. Conversely, no self-identifying Cherokee of the time could abandon tribal identity and be completely accepted as a white U.S. citizen. Degrees of assimilation, and of positions about assimilation, spread across the Cherokee spectrum from purist nativism to complete Westernization. Sequoyah, Boudinot, and Ross ably represent points along this spectrum, and provide useful windows into the complexity of the internal national debates of the Cherokees. The question then becomes not what created the syllabary, but how Cherokee intellectual leaders used the syllabary as a symbol and a tool in the debate regarding assimilation—and, ultimately, removal.

Sequoyah

Sequoyah, also known as George Gist or Guess, was born in the village of Tuskgee, approximately five miles from the Cherokee national capital Echota (near present-day Vonore, Tennessee). His birth date remains uncertain. His father was white, but Sequoyah knew only the company—and the language—of fullblood Cherokees from his early childhood. After serving in a company of Mounted and Foot Cherokees against the Creeks during the War of 1812, Sequoyah returned to his family and to his interrupted endeavor, the creation of a written form of the Cherokee language. Under the treaty of 1817 (an unpopular compact in which Chief Jolly, Sequoyah, and others agreed to voluntary removal) Sequoyah and his family relocated to Arkansas, where he completed the syllabary.

The story of Sequoyah's invention takes on a tragicomic quality considering the enduring effects of the celebrated writing system. Crippled and retired from his trade of silver and blacksmithing, Sequoyah faced social and familial pressure to end his linguistic experiments. Criticized by neighbors and abandoned by friends, he built a separate cabin apart from his home for his seemingly obsessive and eccentric project. His frustrated wife, burdened with his responsibilities as well as her own, even tried to sabotage his work: "To this cabin he confined himself for a year, the whole charge of his farm and family devolving on his wife. When all his friends had remonstrated in vain, his wife went in and capped the climax of her reasonings by flinging his whole apparatus of papers and books into the fire, and thus he lost his first labor."[1]

With years of effort drawing to a close Sequoyah found it necessary to teach another Cherokee his system. When he could find no willing adults to help him prove the utility of his invention, he turned to his daughter, Ahyokeh. The girl, at that time only six years old, not only learned her father's system and demonstrated its use in public, but also proved instrumental in reducing the syllabary from an unwieldy size, nearly 200 characters, to a more manageable 86. Although many standard works today omit any mention of Ahyokeh and her contributions to Sequoyah's syllabary (perhaps because of her death while still a child), the original sources are clear. Even Elias Boudinot, in his 1832 article in *American Annals of Education*, relying on an interview of Sequoyah, explained: "At first, these signs were very numerous, and when he got so far as to think his invention was nearly accomplished, he had about two hundred characters in his Alphabet. By the aid of his daughter, who seemed to enter in the genius of his labors, he reduced them, at last to eighty-six, the number he now uses."[2] Unlike Sequoyah, Ahyokeh did not have the opportunity to enjoy the fruits of her labor. She died at the age of nine.

By having Ahyokeh, and then other youths to whom he taught the revised "Sequoyan," independently translate documents and take dictation before audiences, Sequoyah demonstrated the usefulness of the writing system. Soon knowledge of the syllabary spread among the nearby Cherokees, and those who had scoffed at Sequoyah found their earlier mockery a source of embarrassment. A particularly potent example exists in Elias Boudinot's 1832 article, in which he notes that current Principal Chief (and rival) John Ross was one such scoffer:

> I recollect very well, the first intimation I had of the attempt of Sequoyah to invent an alphabet for the Cherokee language. In the winter of 1822, '23, I was travelling with an intelligent Cherokee, who is now the principal Chief of the nation, on a road leading by the residence of Sequoyah. I had never heard of him until my companion pointed to a certain cabin on the wayside, and observed, 'there, in that house resides George Guess, who has been for the last year attempting to invent an alphabet. He has been so intensely engaged in this foolish undertaking, that he has neglected to do other labor, and permitted his farm to be overrun with weeds and briars.'[3]

It is particularly interesting to note that, in the year Boudinot recalled this anecdote in *American Annals of Education*, Principal Chief John Ross presented Sequoyah with a medal from the Legislative Council of the Cherokee Nation, honoring, in Ross's words, Sequoyah's "transcendant invention."[4]

Use of the syllabary gained nationwide attention at the General Council meeting of New Echota in 1824, when, Boudinot explained, "I saw a number of Cherokees reading and writing in their own language, and in the new characters invented by one of their untutored citizens." Witnessing the success of the system led him to extol

Sequoyah as "the great benefactor of the Cherokees, who, by his inventive powers, has raised them to an elevation unattained by any other Indian nation, and made them a reading and intellectual people."[5] The General Council participants were so impressed with the system that they immediately voted accolades for Sequoyah. Momentum built behind the new system. Because learning to read and write in "Sequoyan" generally took less than one day for Cherokee speakers, last week's students could become the next week's teachers.[6] Missionaries reported that knowledge of the system spread "throughout the nation like fire among leaves."[7] Despite historians' inability to deliver clear statistics on Cherokee literacy, the consensus among historians is that, by 1825, the majority of the Cherokees could read and write using Sequoyah's symbols.[8] In ethnographer James Mooney's words, the whole nation became an academy for the study of the system, and that academy succeeded.[9]

The popularity of the syllabary makes sense. First and foremost, learning the system, whether for its utility or its novelty, was easy for those who already spoke the Cherokee language. Second, the syllabary appealed to diverse ends of the Cherokee political spectrum: the assimilationists, who already knew and appreciated the convenience of a written language because of their familiarity with English, and the purists, who sought to preserve the Cherokee language from extinction in the face of the ever-present English. Learning the language offered a benefit, it seemed, to all Cherokees.

If Sequoyah desired Cherokee unity and resistance—or any political outcome, for that matter—as the direct result of his invention, he was silent about his wishes. Sequoyah's political actions leave a mysterious set of isolated, and contradictory, clues to follow. In one sense he lived the life of a cultural purist. He spoke only Cherokee, served in the military with fullbloods, and located his home near fullbloods. With the exception of his syllabary work, his family life seemed unremarkable. Yet he also isolated himself from the Cherokee Nation, helping to frame the unpopular 1817 treaty against the wishes of then-Principal Chief Pathkiller and voluntarily accepting a kind of exile in Arkansas with a small group of other Cherokees. The life they lived in Arkansas, however, remained a decidedly Cherokee one, with little or no interaction with cultural outsiders. Sequoyah's later actions also reflect the same political ambiguity. After the Trail of Tears in 1838–1839, Sequoyah helped to make peace between the Old Settlers and the newly arrived Cherokees who had endured forced removal. He died while on a quest to locate another group of Cherokees reportedly living in Mexico.

When directly asked the reason for his nearly decade-and-a-half-long pursuit, Sequoyah responded with a story. According to his tale, which was set during a military campaign, a group of Cherokees once captured a prisoner carrying a letter. They could not read it, and the prisoner lied to them about its message. Sequoyah remembered hearing other Cherokees discussing this past event, and the secrets that written words hid from them. Then "the question arose among them, whether this mysterious power of *the talking leaf*, was the gift of the Great Spirit to the white man, or the discovery of the white man himself?"[10] According to his story, Sequoyah believed that white men must have invented writing, and thus other peoples could do so as well. He supposedly thought about this question a great deal but did not pursue it. Only when his leg became crippled and his life necessarily less mobile did he return to the question with renewed enthusiasm, and begin his experiments with the Cherokee syllabary.

Did Sequoyah, a man of obvious intellectual gifts, tackle the challenge of creating a written language because of the story of a prisoner's letter and the reality of his health? Whether the talking leaf story accurately explains how Sequoyah came to create the syllabary, we cannot know. We can know that Sequoyah's control of his writing system ended almost with the moment of its invention. The shift from an oral to a literate Cherokee society fell to the direction of other leaders with political designs far more developed and deliberate than Sequoyah's. The success of the "Sequoyan" system soon left its namesake behind.

Sequoyah's talking leaf story could have ended differently. According to the tale, the soldier carried a letter that the Cherokees could not read. If Sequoyah had interpreted the problem in the story to be the unintelligibility of the soldier's message, his response would have been simply to learn English, as other Cherokees had. Indeed, this position resonated with some of the non-Cherokees who witnessed the syllabary's adoption. Some missionaries, for example, argued that the Cherokee language movement reflected a devolution of Cherokee society, and a threat to their own Christianization efforts. One such missionary wrote: "It is indispensably necessary for their preservation that they should learn our Language and adopt our Laws and Holy Religion ... it seems desirable that their Language, Customs, Manner of Thinking etc. should be forgotten."[11]

But Sequoyah concluded from this story that the Cherokees could make a written language as the whites had done. Whether the tale reflects accurate events or merely Sequoyah's poetic license later in life, the implication of the story remains clear. Sequoyah did not want to be able to communicate with the white soldier. He simply wanted a writing system like the soldier's that belonged to his own people—a separate system to coexist with English. In one sense, this reveals the degree to which Sequoyah had internalized Western values. A written language seemed desirable and necessary, both as a practical tool and as a symbol of a people's accomplishments. But the story also reflects the powerful effect of Cherokee identity on Sequoyah. He did not seek to communicate with the whites, or to make his writing understandable to them. He assumed that the Cherokee culture would remain distinct from U.S. culture, and his system would facilitate the internal communication of one Cherokee to another.

Elias Boudinot

Sequoyah did not follow this rationale to its conclusion, but another Cherokee did. The syllabary's dual promises of civilized communication and cultural exclusion captured the imagination of another visionary, Elias Boudinot, who in turn adopted the syllabary and grafted it to his cause. Unlike the monolingual Sequoyah, Elias Boudinot walked as easily (or perhaps as uneasily) in Bostonian high society as in Cherokee fullblood communities. Born Gallagina or Kiakeena ("Buck") Watie, he left Georgia to study by invitation at the American Board of Commissioners for Foreign Missions school in Cornwall, Connecticut, in 1817. At the time he was twelve or thirteen years old. While en route to his new school Watie met the elderly American Bible Society President and former Continental Congress member, Elias Boudinot. The young Cherokee was so impressed with Boudinot that he immediately renamed himself after the Christian statesman, occasionally spelling his name "Boudinott," when he feared he would cause confusion for a particular audience familiar with both men. At the Foreign Mission school, Boudinot excelled as a student, learning skills such as surveying and studying the classics of philosophy and history. His conversion to Christianity at Cornwall led him to publish letters in the *Religious Remembrancer* and the *Missionary Herald* while still a student. The Foreign Mission school showcased him to locals and visitors alike.

But Boudinot soon learned that he could not completely assimilate into white U.S. society, despite his attempts to do just that. When he successfully proposed marriage to Harriet Ruggles Gold, the daughter of a prominent white physician in Cornwall, the town that had educated, converted, and celebrated Boudinot turned on him. Townspeople marched, protested, and even burned the couple in effigy in the village green. The outrage at the interracial union forced the Foreign Mission school to close its doors permanently within the year. The American Board of Commissioners, in their official annual report, determined that thereafter they would instruct native boys in their own lands, so that they would not fall prey to the vices of "civilized" society. Boudinot, however, did not view his Christian marriage as a vice. He believed that he was betrayed by those he had sought to emulate. Joined by his bride, he went home.

Although Boudinot had kept in contact with his Cherokee culture while in Cornwall and visited Georgia when possible, the world to which he returned was nonetheless a different one than he had known, one now transformed by the Sequoyan system. The syllabary, and the reading and writing it enabled, meant something different to Boudinot than it did to Sequoyah. Where Sequoyah saw a separate creation—the Cherokee's version of the talking leaf—Boudinot saw a step toward civilization. Boudinot had converted not only to Christianity while at Cornwall, but also to European, Judeo-Christian concepts of civilized human progress.

But the very civilization that Boudinot embraced also had hurt him. He had learned from his engagement ordeal that Cherokees could not realistically hope for complete assimilation with the white U.S. mainstream. If civilization was possible for the Cherokees, but assimilation was not, then the Cherokees would have to create their own unique, separate civilization. Such a civilization would possess hybrid traits—Cherokee people and identity, but Western ideas and institutions. He wanted the Cherokees preserved, but transformed. As a student of both worlds and a member of neither, Boudinot was well prepared to articulate his vision.

Nothing symbolized Boudinot's concept of Cherokee civilization better than the syllabary. Post-colonial theorists today would argue that, by imposing Western standards of literacy on their language, the Cherokees were recolonizing themselves, proving how deeply they had internalized Western standards and abandoned their own. This argument has merit, but might be taken a step further. Certainly Boudinot was well aware of what literacy meant in terms of Western civilization. By embracing the syllabary, however, and applying a Western template to a form of Cherokee expression, he was simultaneously elevating the Cherokee image in the eyes of the U.S. mainstream and creating a tongue that was alien and apart from the Americans, capable of preserving Cherokee ideas, traditions, and history for future generations. Sequoyah could not have appreciated the syllabary's unique empowerment—and irony—the way Boudinot could have. With Sequoyah's system the Cherokee Nation maintained its unique tongue, yet accepted its new, written, "civilized" form.

Boudinot soon became integrally involved in its future. In 1825, the General Council of the Cherokee Nation authorized Boudinot to solicit funds for a printing press, Cherokee press types, and a national academy. In his tour of major cities such as Charleston, New York, and Philadelphia, he played the familiar role of the impressive, educated, nonthreatening Cherokee for his white audiences. Of course his nation had accomplished much, but in his fundraising speeches he couched such descriptions in terms of separate Cherokee civilization, not assimilation:

> Yes, methinks I can see my native country, rising from the ashes of her degradation, wearing her purified and beautiful garments, and taking her seat with the nations of the earth.... She will become not a great, but a faithful ally of the United States.... If she completes her civilization—then may we hope that all our nations will—then, indeed, may true patriots be encouraged in their efforts.... But if the Cherokee nation fail in her struggle, if she die away, then all hopes are blasted, and falls the fabric of Indian civilization.[12]

And when listing the achievements of the infant Cherokee civilization, he chose to begin with the syllabary: "There are three things of late occurance [sic], which must certainly place the Cherokee Nation in a fair light, and act as a powerful argument in favor of Indian improvement: First: The invention of letters."[13]

By 1827, the Cherokee Nation seemed to be fulfilling Boudinot's prophecies of future greatness. The National Council had codified law, translated the New Testament into Cherokee, and even ratified a national constitution quite similar to the U.S. Constitution. Boudinot returned from his fundraising campaign a success. In 1827, he accepted the National Council's invitation to edit the nation's first newspaper. Bilingual, like its editor, *The Cherokee Phoenix* would become the mouthpiece for Boudinot's views, and his tool for constructing an image of Cherokee civilization.

Boudinot designed *The Cherokee Phoenix* both to build and to publicize Cherokee progress. Historian Theda Perdue has argued that scholars should be cautious in using *The Cherokee Phoenix* as an ethnohistorical source, because Boudinot was such an unusual and unrepresentative figure. She is quite correct. But *The Phoenix* does offer a window into the mind of Boudinot and therefore into one position on assimilation. *The Phoenix* reflects as much about what Boudinot believed—or wanted—to be true, as what was true. Perdue is accurate in calling the paper an extended "plea for self-preservation."[14] This makes Boudinot's courtship of white readers and then visible use of written Cherokee all the more compelling. Boudinot attempted to construct an image of Cherokee civilization, and used the syllabary as a key means of doing so. To this end, the paper published laws and public documents of the Cherokee Nation, educational material about Cherokee culture, diverse articles of interest, and news from the Cherokee Nation, the United States, and other countries. In fact, in his 1827 prospectus for the paper, Boudinot listed his intended contents:

> As the great object of the *Phoenix* will be the benefit of the Cherokees, the following subjects will occupy its columns.
>
> 1. The laws and public documents of the Nation.
> 2. Account of the manners and customs of the Cherokees, and their progress in Education, Religion and the arts of civilized life; with such notice of other Indian tribes as our limited means of information will allow.
> 3. The principal interesting news of the day.
> 4. Miscellaneous articles, calculated to promote Literature, Civilization, and Religion among the Cherokees.[15]

Dual columns ran, one in English type and the other in Cherokee. To offer an "account of the manners and customs of the Cherokees" and "to promote Literature," Boudinot immediately included a philology section in *The Phoenix* that focused on Sequoyah's syllabary. He entrusted the analysis to his close friend Samuel Worcester, an American Board missionary with whom Boudinot translated the Bible, a hymnal, and tracts into Cherokee. (Worcester is perhaps most well known as the plaintiff on behalf of the Cherokee Nation in the 1832 *Worcester v. Georgia* case. Boudinot was living with Worcester and his wife, awaiting his own house's completion, at the time of his execution, or assassination, in 1839.) The philology section helped readers learn how to use the syllabary. More importantly, Boudinot's constant emphasis on the Sequoyan system suggested to non-Cherokee readers that the Cherokees placed a high value on a literate society. Using Western linguistic analysis to explore the tongue lent it further credibility and respectability. Yet although the language was "civilized"—written, published, and understandable through logical study—it was also exclusive, different, and apart, by the very fact that it was, still, Cherokee.

Boudinot struggled to answer the question of assimilation by building his vision of a Westernized, yet Cherokee, civilization. He knew he had to play to two disparate audiences: the Cherokees, whom he felt needed encouragement, education, and direction; and the whites, whom he knew needed impressive, irrefutable proof of the Cherokees' progress. In this dual quest he often met disappointment. One particularly wounding blow came from the U.S. House of Representatives in its 1830 report from the Committee of Indian Affairs. By this time *The Phoenix* had begun its third year of printing, the Constitution of the Cherokee Nation had entered its fourth year, and the Sequoyan syllabary neared its first decade anniversary. No other native nation could boast of a written language, a national compact, or a national newspaper. Nonetheless, the House Report stated: "The Cherokees are generally understood to have made further advances in civilization than the neighboring nations.... Upon this point the committee feel sensibly the want of that statistical and accurate information, without which, they are aware that they cannot expect their representations to be received...."[16]

Boudinot was incredulous. The U.S. legislature had ignored the very civilization he fought to build and publicize. In the pages of *The Phoenix*, he expressed his anger:

> Here, then is the great mystery—*the committee feel sensibly the want of STATISTICAL and ACCURATE information!* This accounts for their misrepresentations.—But was it impossible to obtain correct statistical information? They thought so we presume, for they sought it "from every *proper source*." ... they seek information from somewhere else, not from documents, and resident whitemen, but from the enemies of the Indian.... [17]

Boudinot redoubled his efforts to make the U.S. mainstream aware of the progress of Cherokee civilization. He continued his work with *The Cherokee Phoenix* and explored other publishing and speaking opportunities as well. As before, his recurring symbol of Cherokee progress remained the syllabary. In his 1832 article in *American Annals of Education*, for example, Boudinot discussed the history of the Sequoyan system and its adoption. While describing the literate nation of the Cherokees, he could not help but lament that: "It is to be regretted that this remarkable display of genius has not been more generally noticed in the periodicals of the day...."[18] The specter of the House Report, and the disregard it reflected, haunted him. As the issue of forced removal loomed larger, Boudinot's preoccupation would shift from helping Cherokee civilization gain recognition to helping it survive. His answer to the assimilation

question—to become like the Westerners yet separate from them—
dictated his answer to the removal question. His solution ultimately
cost him his life.

John Ross

At the same time Boudinot was extolling the Cherokee syllabary
in the pages of *American Annals of Education*, Principal Chief John
Ross was writing words of congratulation to Sequoyah for receiving
an award of national appreciation from the Cherokee National Council. Ironically, John Ross himself had never learned to speak Cherokee, much less read Sequoyah's symbols. Ross fit the profile of those
least likely to learn Cherokee: a small fraction of Cherokee blood,
wealthy, slave owning, involved in commerce and trade principally
outside of the Cherokee Nation. Nonetheless, the figures also suggest
that the political leaders on average knew Cherokee at least as well
as the typical mixed-bloods. Scholars McLoughlin and Conser speculate that "as a ruling elite some of these men learned Cherokee
for political purposes."[19] This was not the case for John Ross.

Only one-eighth Cherokee himself, John Ross was born in 1790
and grew up in the midst of whites as well as fullblood and mixed-
blood Cherokees near present-day Chattanooga, Tennessee. He
attended local festivals and wore traditional Cherokee dress as a boy,
but studied at home with private tutors until he left to attend boarding school. Eventually he relocated among Cherokees in Georgia.
Like Sequoyah, he fought with other Cherokees under U.S. colors
against the Creeks. Ross married a Cherokee and served in a variety
of political positions, finally working up to the positions of president
of the General Council and second principal chief after the death of
Chief Charles Hicks. In 1827 Ross became the first principal chief
elected under the new Cherokee National Constitution. He would be
reelected every four years until his death in 1866.

If, to borrow the current terms of modern U.S. race relations,
Sequoyah represented the isolationist position and Boudinot the
separate-but-parallel position, Ross advocated full integration.
(Sequoyah, Boudinot, and Ross might even be compared with the
later Marcus Garvey, Booker T. Washington, and W. E. B. DuBois,
respectively, as symbolic representatives of the different positions
on assimilation within a minority group.) Ross spent as much time
in Washington, D.C., conducting tribal business as he did in Cherokee lands from the 1810s onward. He appreciated Cherokee
accomplishments on an intellectual level—he even supported

funding the establishment of Boudinot's *Phoenix* and made personal contributions to the paper—but did not connect to such creations as Sequoyah's syllabary on a personal level. Ross's almost austere practicality comes through in his papers. His first written mention of the Sequoyan revolution (excepting his letter to Sequoyah) reads as a list of business accomplished by the National Council. For example, "After the invention of the Cherokee alphabet by George Gist, a native, it was concluded to establish a printing office and issue a paper, in part in the Cherokee language for the diffusion of knowledge among them."[20]

Unlike Boudinot, Ross favored complete assimilation with white U.S. culture. In many ways, Ross was a leader who simply happened to be Cherokee. If he felt a personal burden for a nation, the nation he envisioned had little ethnic, cultural, or racial distinctiveness. His personal life sheds little light onto the baffling racial self-perception—or lack thereof—of John Ross. He had close friends who were fullbloods, such as Major Ridge, the political mentor of Ross's youth. Yet his Cherokee wife, who died on the Trail of Tears, seemed to have touched his life very little. In twenty-six years of marriage, Ross never mentioned her in any of his correspondence or addressed any letters or messages to her, even though because of his career he spent months at a time in Washington, and they had six children together. He seemed to have much more culturally in common with his second wife, a white Quaker woman from Delaware, to whom he was passionately devoted, as his correspondence to her proves.

The difference between Ross's view and Boudinot's would be underscored in the last days of the removal controversy. Ross would fight through the U.S. federal courts to remain on Cherokee land and accept assimilation into the white mainstream. Boudinot would argue that only removal and its opportunity to remain apart from the whites offered Cherokee civilization—and, indeed, Cherokees themselves—a chance for survival. To Ross, then, Sequoyah's syllabary offered little in the way of a useful symbol or tool. The syllabary certainly proved the intellectual abilities of the great Cherokee minds, but that ability simply gave Ross another reason to argue that the Cherokees could survive in the white United States. Ross saw no need to separate Western and Cherokee civilization. He certainly did not want to live in the unassimilated world Sequoyah had recreated in Arkansas.

Ross, Boudinot, and Sequoyah represent points along the spectrum of Cherokee opinion regarding assimilation. But none of the three offers a completely "pure" perspective, untainted by the complex effects of intercultural exchange. Sequoyah, for example, did something unique for a man who preferred the company of full-bloods and spoke only his tribal tongue. He invented his language, giving it a written incarnation. He accepted the white emphasis on literacy and remade his own language in the image of English. In effect, he offered his nation a new tool that, by its very nature, could obliterate the traditional world in which he preferred to live. The assimilationist Ross did not recognize the syllabary's political or intellectual potential, yet he benignly approved of it, supported its use, and then ignored it. The syllabary only became a symbol and a tool in the hands of the bilingual Elias Boudinot, who learned from bitter personal experience that the Cherokee civilization could only survive as a hybrid birth of Cherokee content in Western form, separate from the culture it strove to emulate.

The debate over the origin of the Cherokee syllabary appears terribly simplistic in the light of such complex positions. Clearly the syllabary reflects a series of mixed, even contradictory, impulses—a combination of the Western value of literacy and progress and the Cherokee preservation of an ancient tongue and identity. To separate these impulses and weigh them against each other is to miss the essential issue surrounding the syllabary.

The origin of the Sequoyan revolution can only be found in the gray areas formed by conscious and subconscious cultural interaction. In the broadest sense, then, the Cherokee shift to literacy was both indigenous and imposed. By imposing Western concepts of written literacy on their own language, the Cherokees were actually recolonizing themselves in the pattern of the whites. By applying a Westernized template to their own culture, they made their traditions—their civilization—both understandable and other, alien and apart from those they both copied and defied. This process created the fault lines from which full-scale factions arose during the last days of the removal controversy. These factions played an integral part in the Trail of Tears story.

Notes

1. John Howard Payne, from his interview with Sequoyah, as quoted in Althea Bass, "Talking Stones: John Howard Payne's Story of Sequoya," *Colophon: A Book Collector's Quarterly*, pt. 9 (1932): 12.

2. Elias Boudinot, "Invention of a New Alphabet," in *Cherokee Editor: The Writings of Elias Boudinot*, ed. Theda Perdue (Knoxville: University of Tennessee Press, 1983), pp. 48–58, 53–54.

3. Ibid., p. 54.

4. Letter to George Gist, January 12, 1832, in *The Papers of Chief John Ross*, vol. 1, ed. Gary E. Moulton (Norman: University of Oklahoma Press, 1985), p. 234.

5. Elias Boudinot, untitled article in *American Annals of Education*, April 1, 1832, in *Cherokee Editor*, pp. 48–58, 55, 49.

6. Daniel Butrick's Journal, February 22, 1823, Papers of the American Board of Commissioners for Foreign Missions, Houghton Library, Harvard University.

7. William Chamberlain's Journal, October 22, 1824, Papers of the American Board of Commissioners for Foreign Missions, Houghton Library, Harvard University.

8. William G. McLoughlin and Walter H. Conser, Jr., conducted a statistical analysis of the Federal Cherokee Census of 1835 in 1977. Decidedly problematic, due to unspecific terms (how was literacy measured?), omitted questions, and timing (by 1835, many of the Cherokees had, like Sequoyah, moved west of the Mississippi River and thus were not included), the census nonetheless suggests high rates of literacy: "Percentages of readers of either Cherokee or English were close: 64.7 percent for the less fullblood and 53.9 percent for the more fullblood communities." The census suggested the highest tendencies toward Cherokee reading in the fullblood and mixed blood families (as opposed to families with no fullblood Cherokees). See McLoughlin and Conser, "The Cherokees in Transition: A Statistical Analysis of the Federal Cherokee Census of 1835," *Journal of American History* 64 (December 1977): 678–703, 692.

Willard Walker goes further, however, to speculate "that the Cherokees were 90 percent literate in their native language in the 1830s." See "Notes on Native Writing Systems and the Design of Native Literacy Programs," *Anthropological Linguistics* 2 (1969): 151.

9. James Mooney, *Historical Sketch of the Cherokee* (reprint, Chicago: Aldine, 1975), p. 102.

10. Boudinot, "Invention of a New Alphabet," in *Cherokee Editor*, p. 51. The emphasis belongs to Samuel Lorenzo Knapp, Sequoyah's interviewer. Boudinot quotes passages from the interview throughout his article.

11. John Gambold to Thomas McKenney, August 30, 1824, Moravian Archives, Winston-Salem, NC.

12. Elias Boudinot, "An Address to the Whites," May 26, 1826, in *Cherokee Editor*, pp. 65–83, 77–78.

13. Ibid., p. 74.

14. Theda Perdue, "Rising from the Ashes: *The Cherokee Phoenix* as an Ethnographical Source," *Ethnohistory* 24 (Summer 1977): 207–219, 217.

15. Elias Boudinot, "Prospectus for Publishing in New Echota, in the Cherokee Nation, a Weekly Newspaper to Be Called *The Cherokee Phoenix*," October 1827, in *Cherokee Editor*, pp. 89–90, 90.

16. U.S. House, "Report on Removal," as quoted in *The Cherokee Phoenix*, April 21, 1830, p. 2.

17. Ibid.

18. Boudinot, "Invention of a New Alphabet," in *Cherokee Editor*, p. 49.

19. McLoughlin and Conser, "The Cherokees in Transition," p. 697.

20. John Ross to Lewis Cass, April 22, 1836, in *The Papers of Chief John Ross*, vol. 1, p. 417.

CHAPTER 3

THE JACKSONIAN REVOLUTION, THE U.S. SUPREME COURT, AND POPULAR OPINION

While the Cherokee Nation experienced the changes wrought by the literacy revolution, the ongoing civilization campaign, and the new administration of Principal Chief John Ross—changes that included the ratification of the Constitution of 1827 and the establishment of the Cherokee capital at New Echota—U.S. citizens experienced a revolution, as well: the Jacksonian revolution. Inspired and led by U.S. President Andrew Jackson, this revolution altered the system and psyche of the United States. It was a phenomenon made of contradictions, in one way a grassroots product of the common man, and in another the intensely personal product of an uncommon leader who concentrated power in his own position. Although Cherokee removal took place during the administration of Jackson's successor and former Vice President Martin Van Buren, many consider Jackson to be the single person most responsible for the Trail of Tears.

The Jacksonian Revolution

Andrew Jackson began life as the "common man" he came to personify in the public mind. He was born in 1767 in a rural settlement in the Carolinas, to a family so poverty-stricken that they could not afford a headstone for the grave of his father, who died before his birth. While still a young teenager, he served in the Continental

Army as a courier during the Revolutionary War. When he was captured and held as a prisoner, Jackson refused to clean the boots of a British officer, and in return earned scars he wore throughout his life—and the first of many reasons for his reputation for stubborn courage. One brother, also a prisoner of war, died of smallpox, while Jackson's mother and other brothers died of wartime deprivation. Not only did Jackson emerge from the conflict a young hero, but he also carried with him a potent Anglophobia that later translated into a distrust and even hatred for Eastern and Northern elites in the United States.

Jackson's education was sporadic and incomplete. Nevertheless, as a young man he read law, and he eventually became a successful attorney and planter in the frontier of Tennessee, an owner of a mansion and slaves. Passionately devoted to his wife, Rachel Donelson Jackson, he was known to threaten and fight duels, and even kill to protect her reputation, which at various times was attacked because of the circumstances surrounding her first marriage and subsequent divorce. His experiences seemed to increase his anti-establishment convictions and his dedicated self-reliance. He was a local legend, a self-educated and short-tempered man with ambition, a Tennessee senator and then judge; he gained a national reputation not through his legal practice or domestic adventures, however, but rather through his military service.

As a soldier and commander, Jackson's behavior reflected patterns that followed him to the White House. In 1801 he took the leadership of the Tennessee militia. One of the conflicts in which he was involved was the so-called Red Stick War. The war began as an internal struggle within the Creek Nation between the so-called Red Sticks, Creeks from the Upper Towns who resisted white encroachment and the civilization program, and the so-called White Sticks, those who sought to cooperate with the United States. Eventually this war became complicated by the War of 1812 and the involvement of the Shawnee leader Tecumseh's pan-tribal resistance movement against the United States.

Jackson's leadership in the Red Stick War included attacks on civilian populations, women and children. Just as he showed later with personal disagreements in Washington, he was not content simply to prevail in a conflict: his opposition had to be completely defeated. He proved either unwilling or unable to distinguish between enemy forces who attacked U.S. forts and white communities, and allies who fought alongside him. Among the latter in the war against the Red Stick Creeks in Alabama and Georgia were the friendly Creek faction—the opposing side in this Creek civil war—and

Cherokee forces, most notably The Ridge, who earned his name Major in the conflict, and John Ross. After Jackson and his allies secured victory, he demanded land cessions from friends as well as foes, a total of nearly twenty million acres in all. He held the Red Sticks accountable for their revolt, and the White Sticks accountable for failing to stop it, despite the fact they had tried to do so. The Creek Nation as a whole lost more than half of its ancestral lands.

Jackson's troops similarly disregarded their native brothers in arms; after the watershed victory against the Creeks at the Battle of Horseshoe Bend in 1814, the Cherokees returned home to find their villages had suffered more theft and abuse at the hands of U.S. army allies than they had against their enemy, the Red Stick Creeks.

Jackson's lauded victory in the Battle of New Orleans during— technically, after—the War of 1812 made him a recognized name overnight. Outnumbered two to one against the British, Jackson and his men nonetheless prevailed in that conflict, and Jackson became a Major General. He earned the name Old Hickory because his troops said he was as tough as the tree. His bold and dramatic gestures caught the imagination of many in the United States, as he proved time and time again willing to brave particularly dangerous odds, contradict orders from his superiors, and ignore differences in social status and position, among whites, at least. Such behavior under- scored his admirable bravery and egalitarianism, but also reflected a darker combination of personal emotion—disdain for those he found to be physically weak or culturally different, added to a quick temper and a frank enjoyment of violence—and ideology, namely a firm belief in the gospel of Manifest Destiny, the idea that white U.S. citi- zens had a God-given right to expand throughout and control the continent.

Presidents such as James Monroe found Jackson's service to be both an asset and a liability, as they could claim credit for his stun- ning victories, but they also had to take responsibility for his unau- thorized actions, such as invading lands held by other nations (for instance, his seizure of Spanish Florida), and his killing of various non-U.S. citizens without authorization (for example, his execution of British citizens Robert Ambrister and Alexander Arbuthnot during the First Seminole War of 1818). All of Jackson's choices, whether with or without benefit of official sanction, served the goal of U.S. expansion. Native Americans presented an obstacle to the fulfillment of Manifest Destiny, in his mind; it is no surprise, then, that through- out his military career, Jackson earned and emphasized his reputa- tion as an "Indian fighter," a man who believed creating fear in the native population was more desirable than cultivating friendship.

Jackson's violent impulses led some to question his fitness as a national leader. Thomas Jefferson was one who opposed Jackson's rise in the political sphere:

> I feel much alarmed at the prospect of seeing General Jackson President. He is one of the most unfit men I know of for such a place. He has had very little respect for laws or constitutions, and is, in fact, an able military chief. His passions are terrible. When I was President of the Senate he was a Senator; and he could never speak on account of the rashness of his feelings. I have seen him attempt it repeatedly, and as often choke with rage. His passions are no doubt cooler now; he has been much tried since I knew him, but he is a dangerous man.[1]

Such a dangerous man, however, played well to the tastes of the U.S. public. Jackson's image as the tough, gritty, uncontrollable "Old Hickory" war hero from the frontier played an instrumental role in his eventual election to the presidency. In a four-way split in the election of 1824, he won a plurality of the popular and Electoral College votes. As none of the four presidential candidates won a clear majority, however, the decision went to the U.S. House of Representatives. Because candidate Henry Clay threw his support behind John Quincy Adams, the vote favored Adams over Jackson. Four years later, Jackson defeated Adams in his attempt at reelection in the contentious election of 1828. Jackson received 56 percent of the popular vote. Because suffrage only recently had been expanded by law to include white men without property, the election reflected the fact Jackson had significant support from the non-landowning class, men who aspired to become property holders. Jackson, a Democratic Republican (as opposed to Adams, a National Republican), knew he owed much of his popularity to his "common man" persona. In fact, he threw open the White House to thousands for his inaugural celebration, and provided kegs of whiskey for those outside who could not press their way into the presidential home.

As president, Jackson at times fulfilled his promise as a defender of the common man. For example, he opposed the National Bank, not only because of its dubious constitutionality, but also because, Jackson said, it favored Eastern and wealthy interests over those of the South and West, and those of the frontiersmen. Of course Jackson also suffered from an intense dislike of Nicholas Biddle, the president of the National Bank, which has led some scholars to suggest his position was as much personal as ideological. He did succeed in destroying the institution, however, much to the delight of his supporters.

But Jackson did not always work to give power to the common people; in fact, in many ways, he concentrated power in his own office, or in the national government in general. His "spoils system" plan of patronage meant that many government employees lost their jobs so those positions could be filled by Jackson's friends and supporters, regardless of training and experience. His informal "kitchen cabinet" friends had far more influence on policy than his appointed, credentialed presidential cabinet. He exercised the veto more than any president before him. During the Nullification Crisis, Jackson championed the power of the national government over state governments, threatening the use of troops against South Carolina. Yet, contradictorily, he supported states' rights when he refused to enforce the decision of the U.S. Supreme Court on behalf of the Cherokee Nation against the state of Georgia, opening the door for the Trail of Tears. (This decision did, of course, promise free land to many of the landless men in Georgia who voted for Jackson.)

Despite the power Jackson the Man wielded, he was in some ways not nearly as powerful as Jackson the Idea, as his "common man" egalitarian rhetoric became the inspiration for a variety of reform movements. Grassroots campaigns for temperance, public schools, asylums for the mentally ill, and prison reform gained tremendous strides as they rode the political wave of Jacksonianism. So, too, did the abolitionist movement; William Lloyd Garrison's paper *The Liberator* began publication in 1831, and the American Anti-Slavery Society was established in 1833. The feminist movement followed a similar path, with leaders such as Elizabeth Cady Stanton, Harriet Beecher Stowe, and the Grimke sisters building national support for women's rights, paving the way for the 1848 meeting in Seneca Falls that would produce the "Declaration of Sentiments and Resolutions." Another movement that took shape with the Jacksonian revolution was Transcendentalism, based on the philosophical objective to transcend mere intellect and gain emotional understanding without the hindrances of institutional churches and hierarchies. Transcendentalism produced works against repression and for civil disobedience against unjust laws. Ralph Waldo Emerson and Henry David Thoreau were among the leaders in transcendentalist thought.

Significantly, many of these movements wrestled with questions of justice, fairness, and the dignity of the individual. Because of this, some of the key figures in these reform movements would raise their voices in public protest against Jackson's policy of Indian removal.

The U.S. Supreme Court

The legal story of the Trail of Tears began not with the U.S. Supreme Court, but with various treaties and agreements made by the United States. Perhaps the most important of these was the Compact of 1802, under which the state of Georgia agreed to relinquish to the U.S. national government its claims on western land (including what would become Alabama and Mississippi). In return, the United States agreed to negotiate treaties of sale and removal with the native nations that would, eventually, give Georgia control of all the land within its borders. Such arrangements did not necessarily contradict Jefferson's civilization campaign; in fact, he imagined that most "civilized" tribes would assimilate to the point of disappearance into the main U.S. population. Those separatists who wished to live apart from white U.S. citizens could always choose to leave and go West, Jefferson believed. Was this not one of the options his Louisiana Purchase made possible? The assumption behind this compact, however, was that the native nations would have the choice to negotiate, without coercion or duress.

In 1817, a group of disgruntled Cherokee leaders went against the wishes of the Cherokee National Council and agreed to the Treaty of the Cherokee Agency, which ceded some lands in Tennessee and Georgia, and stipulated that those remaining on the land in question would accept individual land allotments and U.S. citizenship. Although the National Council members called for the treaty's repeal, they only received a revision of the treaty in 1819. In the interim, a number of Cherokees voluntarily moved West into present-day Arkansas and Oklahoma. Most of these Cherokees preferred a more traditional lifestyle; Sequoyah was among their number. The Cherokee National Council was determined that no more land would be surrendered, and the leaders put in writing the decision not to meet with additional treaty commissions and ordered the death penalty for any Cherokee who ceded additional lands.

With the election to the White House of Jackson the "Indian fighter," many Georgians assumed that the moment had arrived to press the state's advantage against the Cherokee Nation. A series of actions by the Georgia legislature made this clear. First, the state redrew its county boundaries to claim Cherokee land. Second, the state extended its laws over the Cherokees, in essence nullifying the Cherokee Nation's sovereignty as a political body. In 1830, Georgia set up a system to redistribute Cherokee land to Georgia citizens. The Cherokees appealed to the national government, claiming that the Georgia state laws, by violating the sovereignty of the Cherokee Nation, also violated international treaties that the United States had made with the Cherokees. In 1831's *Cherokee Nation v. Georgia* decision, the U.S. Supreme Court determined that treaties with the Cherokee Nation were not international treaties because, in the words of Chief Justice John Marshall, they were instead "domestic dependent nations."[2]

While the Georgia state legislature was planning ways to dissolve the Cherokee Nation, the 21st U.S. Congress passed the Indian Removal Act of 1830, and Andrew Jackson enthusiastically signed it into law. This act granted the executive the authority to negotiate land-exchange treaties with native nations residing within the boundaries of the United States. Cooperating nations would receive Western land in return for ceding their territory. Thus "Indian Territory" in present-day Oklahoma was born.

The first treaty under this law was the Treaty of Dancing Rabbit Creek, involving the Choctaws of Mississippi. During Jackson's tenure in office, nearly seventy treaties with Native Americans were ratified. Many of these pertained to land sales; many were coerced, and some were legally illegitimate. As a result, approximately 45,000 members of native nations were relocated to the West during this time, ceding approximately 100 million acres of land for roughly $68 million and 32 million acres in Indian Territory. Eventually the number of the relocated would rise to an estimated 100,000. For this, Jackson suggested the United States should be lauded and the American Indians should be grateful, as he noted in his pleased reaction to the Removal Act:

> Rightly considered, the policy of the General Government toward the red man is not only liberal, but generous. He is unwilling to submit to the laws of the States and mingle with their population. To save him from this alternative, or perhaps utter annihilation, the General Government kindly offers him a new home, and proposes to pay the whole expense of his removal and settlement.[3]

Jackson's public rhetoric about the removal issue alternated between such humanitarian claims and the language of paternalism (painting himself as father and the native nations as children) and racism (invoking descriptive terms related to savagery, decline, and inferiority). Although it would be inaccurate to hold Jackson accountable to twenty-first-century standards, it is significant to note how such rhetoric contrasted sharply with the language used by earlier presidents such as Jefferson.

After the signing of the Removal Act of 1830 and the *Cherokee Nation v. Georgia* disappointment, Cherokee leaders and attorneys searched for a case to bring before the Supreme Court that would not be dismissed. With both the executive and the majority of the legislature behind removal, Cherokee hopes rested in the judicial system. An opportunity arose when Georgia passed an act that required all whites who lived within the Cherokee Nation to apply for a state permit and swear an oath of allegiance to Georgia. The goal of the lawmakers was to identify and remove white supporters of the Cherokees. Many of these were missionaries who lived and worked in the Cherokee Nation. In fact, several ministers from the American Board of Commissioners for Foreign Missions refused to abide by the new Georgia act. For their noncompliance, they were arrested, tried in a Georgia court, convicted, and sentenced to four years of hard labor.

The state offered to pardon the missionaries, but two men, including Elias Boudinot's friend and colleague, Samuel Worcester, declined the offer, in order to test the law—and, in the process, Georgia's claims over the Cherokees. *Worcester v. Georgia* made its way to the U.S. Supreme Court. Now with clear jurisdiction, the Supreme Court was free to decide whether or not Georgia could extend its control into and over the Cherokee Nation. The resulting 1832 majority opinion, once again penned by Chief Justice Marshall, supported the Cherokees. Even as a "domestic dependent nation" rather than a foreign nation, Marshall argued, the Cherokee Nation possessed a right to self-government. According to the decision, previous treaties left the United States with an obligation to protect Cherokee land and sovereignty against any who would infringe against them. No state could simply dissolve what the United States already had recognized and pledged to defend. According to Marshall, Georgia leaders "interfere forcibly with the relations established between the United States and the Cherokee Nation, the regulation of which according to the settled principles of our Constitution, are committed exclusively to the government of the Union."[4]

In the end, however, the Supreme Court's support accomplished nothing for the Cherokee Nation. Jackson refused to enforce the decision, claiming that he would not interfere in state issues. He had, of course, been quite willing to interfere in state issues when it came to the Nullification Crisis, when South Carolina refused to enforce the Tariff of 1828 on the grounds that a state could "nullify" a federal law; Jackson had proven willing then to support national supremacy over states' rights by use of armed force.

But *Worcester* stood in the path of Jackson's vision of Manifest Destiny. The momentum of the Removal Act of 1830, and its promise of American Indian expulsion, ultimately overshadowed the promise of the *Worcester* decision. Cherokee jubilation over the latter was short lived, as the Cherokees realized that the Removal Act, and Jackson's failure to act regarding *Worcester*, signaled that the United States would allow states to coerce native nations into relocation. The U.S. executive and legislature, together with the states, had decided that removal was the only acceptable option for the "Indian problem."

Popular Opinion

Historians agree that a majority of U.S. citizens either supported removal or were indifferent to the issue. Voters had elected Jackson with the general knowledge that a Jackson presidency meant removal of at least the Eastern native nations. Certainly many landless voters, or those with only modest properties, stood to gain from the government's redistribution of American Indian territory, particularly in the South. At no cost to themselves, they could become landholders, when the U.S. government reassigned confiscated Native American land to whites. Moreover, Manifest Destiny was a widespread tenet among U.S. citizens, and not merely the perspective of presidents and lawmakers, and removal clearly fit the Manifest Destiny agenda. Though criticized by some primarily for other policies, Jackson still left his two terms in office a generally popular and loved figure, especially outside of Washington, in the eyes of those "common men" who originally had been his staunchest supporters, further suggesting to historians that removal generally had the active or tacit consent of a majority in the United States.

Jackson's vice president, Martin Van Buren, succeeded Jackson to the presidency with the stated goal of following in Old Hickory's footsteps. Almost immediately saddled with a nation-wide economic crisis that, unfairly perhaps, earned him the nickname of "Martin Van Ruin," Van Buren only held the White House for one term, and he spent most of that time attempting to steer the nation's economy away from complete disaster. Though the Trail of Tears was the direct product of Jackson's policies and actions (or, in the case of *Worcester v. Georgia*, inactions), it took place during Van Buren's administration. It seems Van Buren had neither the intention nor the time to alter the path Jackson had prepared for the Cherokee Nation. Furthermore, Van Buren's defeat in his second campaign was far from a condemnation of removal, because the winning candidate, William Henry Harrison, was as famed an "Indian fighter" as Jackson himself, and offered no real alternative to Jackson's policies regarding Native America.

Overt supporters of removal existed outside of Georgia and Washington, D.C., as well. One of the best known and most visible was Lewis Cass, who served as governor of the Michigan Territory from 1813 to 1831. In addition to his work in politics, Cass also was a writer who published articles in national magazines and literary reviews. A number of his works expressed opinions about the condition and future of the native nations. The most influential appeared in 1830 in the *North American Review*; in this fifty-nine page article he systematically articulated his reasons for supporting removal. At the heart of his essay was a warning that underscored the anxieties of the white mainstream: the Cherokee Nation's assertion of sovereignty—for that matter, of existence—would lead to similar claims by other groups, and the conflict would never end except with bloodshed. Overlooking the fact that the Cherokee Nation predated the state of Georgia, Cass used his argument about the "slippery slope" of allowing Cherokees and others to claim and maintain territory in the East to play on the worst racial fears of his audience, insinuating that eventually these Eastern natives would seek war against whites. Cass suggested that American Indians eventually might attempt conquest against their white neighbors if allowed to remain east of the Mississippi, a prediction he seemed to make without any sense of irony. Cass's defense of removal gained him increased national visibility. He eventually rose to the position of U.S. senator (serving as president pro tempore of the Senate during the Thirty-third Congress) and secretary of state under President James Buchanan.

Not everyone in the United States supported the removal policy, however. Many leaders of "Jacksonian" reform movements were particularly disturbed by U.S. policy toward American Indians. Catherine Beecher, women's advocate and founder of the American Woman's Educational Association, penned her "Circular Addressed to Benevolent Ladies of the U. States" on Christmas day in 1829. She called upon all women to recognize the United States' duties as protector and defender of the native nations. Pointing out the various successes of the civilization campaign, and the accomplishments of the Native Americans, Beecher argued that both Christianity and humanitarianism required that women oppose the policy of removal. Such a plan of action, she argued, would mean extinction for its victims. Her concerns were not only for the natives themselves; she considered God to be an avenger of wrongs, and she feared for her country's future if it committed what she considered to be a grave injustice.

One of the most visible figures in the Transcendentalist movement, Ralph Waldo Emerson, published an open letter to President Martin Van Buren in 1838 specifically about the plight of the Cherokee Nation. He, like Beecher, praised the many achievements of the native people; also, like Beecher, he warned that such an act would have repercussions not only for the removed, but also for the remover: "However feeble the sufferer and however great the oppressor, it is in the nature of things that the blow should recoil upon the aggressor."[5]

Not all of those opposed to removal were known primarily as members of new Jacksonian movements. Jeremiah Evarts, the leader of the American Board of Commissioners for Foreign Missions, presented a series of twenty-four essays in the Washington publication *National Intelligencer* in 1829 known as "Essays on the Present Crisis in the Condition of the American Indians." Writing under the pen name "William Penn"—thus invoking the founder of the Pennsylvania Colony, who was remembered as a champion of liberty, peace, and conscience—Evarts methodically explored the past history of U.S.–American Indian legal interactions. His detailed analysis exposed the fact that Georgia had no viable claim to Cherokee lands, leading him to conclude that "They [the Cherokees] have not intruded upon our territory, nor encroached upon our rights. They only ask the privilege of living unmolested in the places where they were born, and in possession of those rights, which we have acknowledged and guaranteed...."[6]

Protest even came from unexpected places. Tennessee congressman and contemporary legend, Davy Crockett, had his own reputation as an "Indian fighter"; in fact, he had fought with Andrew Jackson—and John Ross and The Ridge—against the Creeks during the Red Stick War. His national political career seemed tied to Jackson's administration and the frontier mentality it represented, including the idea of Manifest Destiny. Crockett broke ranks with Jackson, however, over the Indian Removal Act of 1830, which he firmly opposed. He recognized the political danger he faced by challenging one of Jackson's signature policies. As he said in his autobiography,

> His [Jackson's] famous, or rather I should say infamous, Indian bill was brought forward, and I opposed it from the purest motives in the world. Several of my colleagues got around me, and told me how well they loved me, and that I was ruining

myself. They said this was a favourite measure of the president, and I ought to go for it. I told them I believed it was a wicked, unjust measure, and that I should go against it, let the cost to myself be what it might; that I was willing to go with General Jackson in everything that I believed was honest and right; but further than this I wouldn't go for him, or any other man in the whole creation. I voted against this Indian bill, and my conscience yet tells me that I gave a good honest vote, and that I believe will not make me ashamed in the day of judgment.[7]

Crockett eventually was defeated twice in his bids for reelection, in large part because of the concerted effort of the Jackson camp to punish him for his opposition. Crockett responded by leaving politics altogether and joining the fight for Texas independence, where his part in the ill-fated Battle of the Alamo became legendary.

The Cherokees were not alone in opposing what would become the Trail of Tears. But while some intellectual, activist, and political leaders gave reasons why the United States should change the direction in which its policies were heading, many others promoted and defended plans for removal. In the end, the ears that mattered were deaf to protests.

Notes

1. In *The Writings of Thomas Jefferson*, vol. 10, ed. Paul Leicester Ford (New York: G. P. Putnam's Sons, 1899), p. 331.

2. *Cherokee Nation v. State of Georgia*, available at http://caselaw.lp.findlaw.com/scripts/getcase.pl?navby=case&court=us&vol=30&invol=1 (accessed January 12, 2006).

3. See the Primary Documents section.

4. See the Primary Documents section.

5. See the Primary Documents section.

6. William Penn [Jeremiah Evarts], "A Brief View of the Present Relations between the Government and People of the United States and the Indians within Our National Limits," quoted in *The Cherokee Removal: A Brief History with Documents*, ed. Theda Perdue and Michael D. Green, 2nd ed. (New York: Bedford/St. Martin's, 2005), pp. 105–110, 110.

7. Davy Crockett, *A Narrative of the Life of Davy Crockett, by Himself* (Lincoln: University of Nebraska Press, 1987), pp. 205–206.

CHAPTER 4

POLITICAL PARTIES AND THE TREATY OF NEW ECHOTA

The traditional history textbook story of the Trail of Tears often focuses on U.S. Supreme Court decisions, Congressional acts, and, ultimately, the personality and power of President Andrew Jackson. To be sure, in the final analysis of this complex event, the U.S. executive branch acted, leaving the Cherokees to play the role of the "acted upon." Within the Cherokee Nation, however, the removal crisis triggered an internal political showdown, one with drastic and bloody consequences. Certainly many influences affected this debate: property holdings, political aspirations, kin loyalties. But the dramatic factionalization of the Cherokee Nation in the 1830s can also be seen as the clash between two specific visions of the Cherokees' future. By 1832, the most popular figure in the Cherokee Nation, Principal Chief John Ross, and the most visible figure in the Cherokee Nation, *Phoenix* editor Elias Boudinot, championed opposing visions of what the Cherokees had accomplished and what they could become. Parties grew around both men's ideas, eventually carrying them further than either leader could alone. The internal Cherokee schism during the removal crisis, then, reflected nothing less than two contradictory understandings of Cherokee civilization.

The removal question, a silent backdrop to U.S.–American Indian interactions even before Jefferson, recaptured Cherokee attention by the late 1820s. The U.S. national government tried many means of convincing Cherokees to move, even paying some of those who had voluntarily relocated in the West to return East to advertise their satisfaction. Such ploys led Boudinot to complain: "Why are these inter-meddling Cherokees thrust in amongst us and paid by the United States when they are unwelcomed, and possess no right in this country?"[1] Fearing that a few unauthorized Cherokees might find the U.S. pressure persuasive, a concerned Cherokee National Council passed a law in 1829 making cession of tribal land a capital offense. This law would later haunt Cherokees on both sides of the partisan schism of the 1830s.

Political Parties

The decision seemed to signal a halt to threats against Cherokee autonomy. After all, the Indian Removal Act permitted only consensual, treaty-based relocation, and the Cherokee national government had made it clear that the Cherokees had no interest in moving west en masse. The *Worcester* decision protected the Cherokees from state interference. The nation appeared safe, then, from both U.S. and Georgia government action. Upon hearing the decision, Boudinot wrote his brother Stand Watie:

> It is a glorious news. The laws of the State are declared by the highest judicial tribunal in the Country null and void. It is a great triumph on the part of the Cherokees so far as the question of their rights were concerned. The question is for ever settled as to who is right and who is wrong, and the controversy is exactly where it ought to be and where we have all along been desirous it should be.[2]

He went on to write: "And I will take upon myself to say that this decision of the Court will now have a most powerful effect on public opinion. It creates a new era on the Indian question."[3] The new era that followed, however, was not the one Boudinot anticipated.

Boudinot embraced the news as a promise that the Cherokees would, indeed, be left alone to pursue their own internal civilization campaign. But the more politically savvy John Ross, who had spent the duration of the trials in Washington, D.C., met the decision with wariness. He knew that the election of 1832 brought the enforcement of the *Worcester* decision into question. The funds and time spent going through the U.S. judicial system—and winning—might still be for naught. He believed, "It was however the duty of the Court to have done what they did, but the executive would not sustain them."[4]

Ross was correct. Andrew Jackson's reelection brought him back to the White House with a solid mandate from U.S. citizens.

When the state of Georgia refused to submit voluntarily to the Supreme Court's decision, Jackson said nothing. Most of the U.S. public seemed satisfied with Jackson's position. In fact, when Worcester considered appealing to Marshall and the Court, the Prudential Committee of the American Board of Commissioners for Foreign Missions not only advised him against an appeal, but asked Worcester to convince the Cherokees to accept removal and move west. The Cherokees had won the Worcester case and yet still lost it. Jackson's passive approval of Georgia's defiance sealed the Cherokees' defeat.

By any name—nation-building, consensus, or conscious civilization campaign—the Cherokee Nation had achieved unity during the five years prior to *Worcester*, exemplified by the support of the national constitution of 1827, the syllabary movement, and of course *The Cherokee Phoenix*. After Jackson ignored the U.S. Supreme Court's *Worcester* decision, this unity crumbled.

Ross and Boudinot responded to the crisis according to their understandings of and hopes for Cherokee civilization. Ross, still advocating the assimilation of the Cherokees with the dominant U.S. culture, concentrated on protecting Cherokee property and wealth from Georgia citizens and others who encroached upon Cherokee territory for land and gold. He understood that respect and power in the United States required that his people maintain their status as producers, as merchants, as planters, and as landowners. As long as the Cherokees maintained their wealth, they retained leverage. Boudinot, conversely, felt that Cherokee progress was impossible in the political climate created by President Jackson and Governor George Gilmer. The Cherokees could not progress while suffering oppression at the hands of Georgia. The separate Cherokee civilization he dreamed of, it seemed, would have to be geographically separated from the U.S. mainstream as well as symbolically so.

Ross and Boudinot had joined forces to create and fund *The Cherokee Phoenix* in 1827. It had served both of their purposes, advertising Cherokee accomplishments and nurturing a Cherokee national consciousness. But after *Worcester*, Boudinot felt that the Cherokees had no other choice than to relocate west. This position placed him in direct opposition to the principal chief. Because the Cherokee national government financially supported *The Phoenix*, and because Ross served as the head of that government, his pressure could effectively force Boudinot from the editorship. So when Boudinot announced that he had decided to support removal, the editor lost his paper. Boudinot resigned under pressure with little attempt to hide his reason:

> Were I to continue as Editor, I should feel myself in a most pe-
> culiar and delicate situation. I do not know whether I could, at
> the same time, satisfy my own views, and the authorities of this
> nation.... I could not consent to be the conductor of the paper
> without having the right and privilege of discussing these impor-
> tant matters....[5]

Upon losing *The Phoenix*, Boudinot devoted his time to the only
alternative he could see to preserve the emerging Cherokee civilization he had championed. With uncle Major Ridge, cousin John
Ridge, brother Stand Watie, and others, Boudinot formed a political
group to seek removal actively. In the past, each had articulated anti-
removal sentiments. But the times, they felt, had changed, and relocation provided the only defense against destruction. Not long after
Boudinot's public resignation from *The Phoenix*, both Major and John
Ridge lost their positions on the Cherokee National Council,
impeached by petition for "maintaining opinions and a policy to ter-
minate the existence of the Cherokee community on the lands of our
fathers."[6] The petition was presented by none other than Elijah
Hicks, Boudinot's replacement as the editor of *The Phoenix*.

Considering their intellectual positions, the actions of Boudinot
and Ross appear ironic. Despite his assimilationist ideas, Ross nonetheless treated the emergence of the two political parties in a traditional Cherokee manner. In the pre-Contact or pre-acculturation
Cherokee system, minority dissenters would withdraw from the dialogue, offering no participation or support and yet also offering the
chance for the majority to present a unified front. The value Cherokees placed on consensus necessitated such withdrawal. When the
opposition did not withdraw, Ross and his colleagues tried to coerce
its silence. Historian Barbara F. Luebke paints this opposition as follows: "Ross's position—that the tribally funded newspaper must reflect
the views of the tribal government—and Boudinot's adherence to a basic premise of a democratic press—the freedom and necessity of
expressing contrary points of view—had come to an inevitable conclusion."[7] Meanwhile, Ross attempted a series of stalling measures in the
form of appeals, letters, and speeches in the hopes that U.S. leaders
would grow tired of the removal controversy when it became clear
that the Cherokees were unwilling to relocate and when Georgia gold
fever died a natural death. As the National (or Ross) Party leader, Ross
sought to limit confrontation, buy time, and find a means to either
quiet or build consensus with the Treaty (or Ridge-Boudinot) Party.

Boudinot and his colleagues, seeking to separate themselves
from U.S. political and cultural domination, nevertheless chose a

decidedly aggressive and confrontational manner of vocalizing their dissent, as if mimicking the U.S. political culture rather than their traditional one. Where Ross sought the patience to wait, Boudinot felt it necessary to act immediately if Cherokee lives and culture were to be saved. As Ross tried to act in a calm and "civilized" manner, then, Boudinot ached to act quickly—even as a renegade—in order to save Cherokee civilization.

The Treaty of New Echota

And renegade he was. Boudinot's Treaty Party had few supporters. Of the roughly fifteen thousand Cherokees still within the national dialogue—excluding those who had chosen to move west, passed altogether into the U.S. culture, or already fled to the mountains—historian William G. McLoughlin estimates the number of Treaty Party followers as a mere seventy-five.[8] Boudinot himself only claimed fifty.[9] Clearly, most Cherokees supported Ross's desire to remain on historic Cherokee land.

After a bipartisan delegation suggested by Ross and including Treaty Party members failed to yield satisfactory negotiations with the United States, the Treaty Party turned to their own plans. Jackson, sensing an opportunity, sanctioned a special commissioner, Reverend John F. Schermerhorn, to pursue a treaty. Schermerhorn invited the Cherokees to a meeting in New Echota. The U.S. government, Schermerhorn noted in his invitation, would consider Cherokee absence as acquiescence to any agreement reached.[10] In the meantime, Stand Watie and some of his forces had "liberated" the printing equipment of the failed *Phoenix* from Elijah Hicks's house on behalf of the Treaty Party. Boudinot then translated Schermerhorn's invitation into Cherokee and printed it on the stolen press.

Few Cherokees responded to Schermerhorn's call. The Treaty Party, without benefit of elected position or authorization, therefore proceeded to negotiate with Schermerhorn unhindered by Ross or the National Council. On December 29, 1835, twenty Cherokees including Boudinot signed the treaty that sold the Cherokee lands in the East and agreed to relocate all tribe members west of the Mississippi River. Boudinot argued that Ross had abdicated his role as leader by failing to orchestrate a legal removal. If Ross would not facilitate removal, then someone had to step forward and do so. Boudinot painted himself and his fellow party members as patriots, willing to risk their lives by making an unpopular choice for the preservation of their people, saying, "I know I take my life into my hand. . . . We can die, but the great Cherokee Nation will be saved. They will not be annihilated; they can live. Oh, what is a man worth who will not dare to die for his people? Who is there here that would not perish, if this great nation may be saved?"[11] Major Ridge agreed on the unpopularity of signing the treaty, telling one U.S. colonel: "I expect to die for it."[12] Their words soon proved prophetic.

The U.S. national government, through the sanctioned person of Schermerhorn, accepted the New Echota Treaty as binding on the whole Cherokee Nation. Ross and the National Council, however, who first learned of the compact only through secondhand accounts, knew the treaty to be illegal and illegitimate. Ross fought the treaty, appealing to the U.S. Congress. He renewed his pleas during the Van Buren presidency, though he lamented from Washington that "the President [Van Buren] is unwilling to take the responsibility on himself of doing away that which has been done by General Jackson."[13] He argued that Boudinot and his compatriots had no authority to make the treaty, for they were not elected and they had no majority support within the nation. Boudinot readily admitted to these charges. He justified his actions in terms of patriotism, enlightenment, and civilization, portraying a Brutus-like image of himself as the disinterested caretaker of the national interest willing to do his necessary but unpleasant duty because others lacked the foresight to do so:

> [W]e cannot conceive of the acts of a *minority* to be so reprehensible or unjust as are represented Mr. Ross. If one hundred persons are ignorant of their true situation, and are so completely blinded as not to see the destruction that awaits them, we can see strong reasons to justify the action of a minority . . . to do what the majority *would do* if they understood their condition— to save a *nation*. . . .[14]

Boudinot did not endear himself with Ross or his supporters by using this kind of language.

As the Treaty Party members relocated in the West, Ross continued to fight against the treaty in the East, instructing the Cherokees to continue planting as usual while he worked in Washington to undo the New Echota damage. But despite his efforts forcible removal began. The methods were both brutal and inefficient. In two months' time, U.S. General Winfield Scott had already exceeded the original U.S. budget for Cherokee removal, with a year's efforts still ahead. Ross knew defeat. He was himself evicted from his home when a Georgian drew his holdings in the state's Cherokee land lottery. He then recast his demands, asking to take charge of removal himself. The U.S. national government agreed to turn over the disastrous project and Ross quickly reorganized and refinanced removal, increasing both the humanitarianism and efficiency of the process.

Perhaps the swift retreat and obvious absence of the Treaty Party following the New Echota Treaty meant doom for its members. Boudinot envisioned himself as the preserver of a separate Cherokee civilization. He proved willing to orchestrate an unpopular, even illegal, treaty in the belief that he saw the situation more clearly than the nation's leader or the nation's majority. But when the time came for the treaty to be implemented, Boudinot and his fellow party members had already gone to the West. They did write encouraging, descriptive letters about life on the other side of the Mississippi. But they did not stay with their fellow Cherokees and help deliver their nation through the process that they themselves had begun. If Boudinot was Brutus, reckless with devotion for Rome, then this Brutus plotted Caesar's death, but disappeared before unsheathing his blade.

Ross, on the other hand, did not share Boudinot's vision of a separate Cherokee civilization. He imagined a gradual assimilation with U.S. culture. In his personal life, he lived it. In his political life, he showed remarkable faith in U.S. procedure, arguing earnestly before Congress even after witnessing the *de facto* stillbirth of the *Worcester* decision. He blamed the men, not their laws and system. And Ross lost. He lost his fight for *Worcester*, he lost his fight against the New Echota Treaty, and he lost his fight for Cherokee lands.

Despite his solid refusal to support removal, however, Ross eventually became its final architect. In essence, he finished what Boudinot began. When his people suffered, he abandoned his principled arguments in favor of practical aid. The Cherokees responded with an outpouring of support that did not end until his death in 1866, while still holding office as principal chief. The people held him accountable for neither his negotiation failures in Washington nor the Trail of Tears itself. They rewarded him for his intentions.

The same was not true for Elias Boudinot. Despite his intentions and those of his fellow party members, many Cherokees blamed the Treaty Party not only for the loss of the Eastern lands but also for the incredible death toll of removal itself. As one missionary among the Cherokees put it, "All the suffering and all the difficulties of the Cherokee people charge to the accounts of Messrs. Ridge and Boudinot."[15] Just as Cherokee public opinion exonerated Ross, it also demanded justice—or vengeance—against the Treaty Party.

Those who sought retribution found justification in the 1829 Cherokee law that made ceding land without authorization a capital offense. It had been, in fact, Major Ridge who had championed the law in the National Council, and John Ridge who actually penned it. The signers were well aware that their consent to the New Echota Treaty carried with it a death sentence, and they even communicated this to Schermerhorn, who indicated: "These men, before they entered upon their business, knew they were running a dreadful risk, for it was death by their laws...."[16] Cherokee justice found its face in a curious cultural schizophrenia that Boudinot would have appreciated in the abstract. Conspirators, former members of the National Council and Ross family members among them, met to read this law and determine how the sentence against the Treaty Party could be dealt quickly. On the one hand, it was a Westernized concern for a law passed beneath a constitutional government. On the other, the meeting was a traditional Cherokee affair. Those who met determined that the four Treaty Party members most responsible for New Echota included Elias Boudinot, Stand Watie, Major Ridge, and John Ridge, and they made certain that their fellow conspirators included members of the victims' clans, to ensure that no clan vengeance would be invoked after the "executions." After both constitutional and clan law seemed satisfied in the minds of the conspirators, they moved.

Allen Ross, son of the chief, stayed at home with his father on June 22, 1839, to distract and insulate him from the day's events, of which he was unaware. (Ironically enough, only two days earlier, on June 20, Sequoyah and Jesse Bushyhead, both prominent "Old Settlers," or Cherokees that had removed to the West prior to forced removal, issued a joint statement calling for an end to partisanship and a new, unified general council.) The other conspirators acted. They found Major Ridge on the road, riding alone. He died instantly from five bullets. They pulled his son John from his bed and stabbed him twenty-six times in front of his family, then tortured him as he bled to death. They waited until Boudinot left his friend Samuel Worcester's home. Then they stabbed him in the back and, as he lay dying, split his head open with repeated tomahawk blows and then drastically mutilated his body. By noon on that Saturday, all three men were dead.

The secrecy with which the conspirators planned allowed them to coordinate multiple, simultaneous strikes. Members of each of the victims' households immediately sent warning to the other Treaty Party leaders after discovering the murders, only to find that their messages were too late. Only Stand Watie received warning in time.

Upon hearing of his brother's death, he immediately took flight and gathered remainders of the Treaty Party supporters. Thus protected, he issued a reward for his brother's killers and publicly blamed Ross for the day's events. Yet despite his threats against Ross (including one abortive attempt to lead military forces against the principal chief) and his appeals to the United States for satisfaction, Watie never found those responsible for the June 22 assassinations. The Cherokees as a whole seemed satisfied, even pleased, that the lives were taken. Ross's tenuous attempts at an inquiry were thwarted, and soon forgotten. A cultural consensus protected the perpetrators. After all, the killers were, in essence, carrying out not only codified law, but also older Cherokee law as well as the preference of the majority.[17]

According to surviving accounts, Ross felt no satisfaction in the death of the opposition. On a personal level the loss of Major Ridge, the political mentor of Ross's early days, proved particularly hard for him to accept. (It was reported that, upon hearing of The Ridge's death, Ross said: "Once I saved Ridge at Red Clay, and I would have done so again had I known of the plot."[18]) His son's involvement in the conspiracy added another dimension to the tragedy. Politically, the assassinations spawned even greater tribal divisions and violent unrest. Perhaps most importantly to the assimilationist Ross, the murders horrified the U.S. public, furthering the popular stereotype of the savage, bloodthirsty Indian he had fought so hard to overturn during his tenure as chief and his battles in Washington. The leadership of the opposing party might have been neutralized, but the fact left Ross little relief.

The contradictions and nuances of the internal Cherokee schism during the removal crisis defy easy explanation. Too many subtle forces compete for causality, each pointing to the complex realities created by the intellectual, social, and political relationships of the United States and Cherokee Nation. Ross, the assimilationist, believed in Western civilization, in the U.S. system even when it betrayed him, and in the economic processes that brought him and his people wealth and power. When land and gold and jealousy became too tempting for Georgians, they threatened Ross's vision of a civilized Cherokee Nation. He fought for it through the U.S. system, and yet also proved eminently Cherokee in his coercion of minority dissent. Those who followed him forgave him. They also avenged their pain in a deadly strike borne of both constitutional and clan law.

Conversely, Boudinot imagined a separate Cherokee civilization, Westernized, yet Cherokee. The Worcester aftermath solidified his mistrust of the United States, and he believed the only answer was removal. So, against tribal traditions of withdrawal and clan law, he vocalized his dissent. When Ross would not act, Boudinot even illegally signed away his people's birthright. To the end, Boudinot could not understand the national hatred the Cherokees developed for their former editor and his party:

> The Treaty Party is not to blame for this—We sounded the alarm in time—we called upon the authorities of the nation to see to what these matters were tending—to save the nation by timely action—we asked, we entreated, we implored.—But we were met at the very threshold as enemies of our country.[19]

The only constant in the tale remains two opposing visions of Cherokee civilization: Ross's assimilation and Boudinot's separate Cherokee world. They led to distinctly different answers to the removal question. Ross's view maintained majority support, but Boudinot's became implemented. Neither man, and neither view of the Cherokee future, could ever have anticipated the carnage of the Trail of Tears. After removal, it is difficult to say which vision of civilization won the debate. Ross remained in control, and the nation ratified a new U.S.-styled Cherokee National Constitution. But the tribe faced isolation. Geographically, Indian Territory lay at the periphery of "civilized" America. In the minds of U.S. citizens after the killings of Boudinot and both Ridges, the Cherokees were now even more different and other, savages who had approved of a gruesome bloodbath in the name of law. Ross had his Western institutions. Boudinot had his separation. And the Cherokees would have civil war.

Notes

1. Elias Boudinot, *The Cherokee Phoenix*, August 20, 1828, p. 2.

2. Elias Boudinot to Stand Watie, March 7, 1832, quoted in *Cherokee Cavaliers: Forty Years of Cherokee History as Told in the Correspondence of the Ridge-Watie-Boudinot Family*, ed. Edward Everett Dale and Gaston Litton (Norman: University of Oklahoma Press, 1939), pp. 4–7, 4–6.

3. Ibid., p. 6.

4. John Ross to William Wirt, June 8, 1832, in *The Papers of Chief John Ross*, vol. 1, ed. Gary E. Moulton (Norman: University of Oklahoma Press, 1985), pp. 244–246, 245.

5. He went on to write: "I love my country and I love my people, as my own heart bears me witness, and for that very reason I should think it my duty to tell them the whole truth, or what I believe to be the truth."

Elias Boudinot, *The Cherokee Phoenix*, August 11, 1832, p. 1. Elijah Hicks assumed Boudinot's position as editor. The paper was short-lived after Boudinot's departure, however, and Hicks published its last issue on May 31, 1834.

6. Benjamin Currey, September 15, 1834, quoted in Thurman Wilkins, *Cherokee Tragedy: The Ridge Family and the Decimation of a People*, 2nd ed. (Norman: University of Oklahoma Press, 1986), p. 263.

7. Barbara F. Luebke, "Elias Boudinot and 'Indian Removal'," in *Outsiders in Nineteenth-Century Press History: Multicultural Perspectives* (Bowling Green, OH: Bowling Green State University Popular Press, 1995), pp. 115–144, 141.

8. William C. McLoughlin, *Cherokee Renascence in the New Republic* (Princeton, NJ: Princeton University Press, 1986), p. 450.

9. Elias Boudinot, "To the Public," in *Cherokee Editor: The Writings of Elias Boudinot*, ed. Theda Perdue (Knoxville: University of Tennessee Press, 1983), pp. 159–162, 162.

10. 5th Congress, 2nd session, Senate Document 120 (Serial 315): 533-534; 5th Congress, 2nd session, Senate Document 121 (Serial 315): 29; and 5th Congress, 2nd session, Senate Document 120 (Serial 315): 518, quoted in Wilkins, *Cherokee Tragedy*, p. 281.

11. Elias Boudinot, *Cartersville Courant*, March 26, 1885, p. 1.

12. Thomas L. McKenney, *Memoirs, Official and Personal: With Sketches of Travels among the Northern and Southern Indians*, vol. 1 (New York: Paine and Burgess, 1846), p. 265.

13. John Ross to George Lowrey, January 27, 1838, in *The Papers of Chief John Ross*, vol. 1, pp. 584–586, 584.

14. Boudinot, "To the Public," in *Cherokee Editor*, pp. 159–162, 162.

15. Elizur Butler to Greene, August 2, 1838, quoted in Wilkins, *Cherokee Tragedy*, p. 328.

16. John F. Schermerhorn, quoted in William G. McLoughlin, *After the Trail of Tears: The Cherokees' Struggle for Sovereignty, 1839–1880* (Chapel Hill: University of North Carolina Press, 1993), p. 13.

17. McLoughlin, *After the Trail of Tears*, p. 17.

18. Edmund Schwarze, *History of the Moravian Missions among Southern Indian Tribes of the United States* (Bethlehem, PA: Times Publishing, 1923), p. 191.

19. Boudinot, "To the Public," in *Cherokee Editor*, pp. 159–162, 162.

CHAPTER 5

THE TRAIL OF TEARS

The U.S. Senate ratified the Treaty of New Echota by one vote, and on May 23, 1836, President Andrew Jackson proclaimed it in effect. This set the deadline for the voluntary exodus of nearly twenty thousand Cherokees from their homes to lands across the Mississippi River for May 23, 1838. After that date, those who remained would be moved by force. The U.S. secretary of war told John Ross that Jackson no longer recognized any government among the Eastern Cherokees, and neither Ross nor anyone else would be allowed to challenge further the legitimacy of the removal treaty. At the same time, congressmen and community leaders urged Ross not to give up hope, but rather to trust that the system would work, and justice would prevail, before the deadline for relocation arrived.

Immediate action on behalf of the treaty did not come easily. General John Ellis Wool was the commander of the U.S. troops originally ordered to enforce the Treaty of New Echota. When he arrived to begin the process of disarming the Cherokees, he was met with a memorial signed by council members, protesting both the treaty itself and the plan for disarmament that followed from it. When he attended a council meeting in September 1836, he learned even more about the Cherokee majority's side of the New Echota story:

> [I]t is, however, vain to talk to people almost universally opposed to the treaty and who maintain that they never made such a treaty. So determined are they in their opposition that not one ... would receive either rations or clothing from the United States lest they might compromise themselves in regard to the treaty.... The whole scene since I have been in this country has been nothing but a heartrending one, and such a one as I would be glad to get rid of as soon as circumstances will permit.[1]

Wool asked to be relieved of his mission, and he was.

Brigadier General R.G. Dunlap led his Tennessee troops to begin building stockades for the use of the U.S. soldiers who would enforce removal, and containment pens to hold the Cherokees who did not plan to leave voluntarily. The problem was that the construction sites put Dunlap and his men close to Cherokee communities and homes. They talked; they socialized. The contrast between the sophistication of the Cherokees—many of the young girls had been educated formally by Christian missionaries—and the crudeness of the wooden pens that were meant for their imprisonment soon struck the Tennessee forces. At length, Dunlap threatened to resign his commission rather than continue to assist in preparations for removal, claiming that enforcing the Treaty of New Echota would dishonor both his men and his home state.

Meanwhile, only about two thousand Cherokees, less than 15 percent of the Cherokee Nation, left of their own accord to join the "Old Settlers" in Indian Territory in the West. Among them were members of the Treaty Party. Despite the fact that his men in the field balked at their orders, Jackson remained firm. The Treaty of New Echota would be implemented. He gave instructions that no one have additional communications with John Ross, in speech or writing, about the treaty. After Jackson served out his second term in the White House, his vice president and hand-picked successor, Martin Van Buren, began his administration in March 1837, making it clear that he had every intention of following Jackson's precedents and implementing Jackson's policies.

In August 1837, the Cherokees gathered by the thousands at Red Clay, Tennessee, which served as the seat of government in the place of New Echota after the state of Georgia forbid the Cherokee Council to meet. At this meeting a U.S. agent sent for the purpose made a speech in which he tried to convey that resistance to removal was useless. The talk in question did not manage to end opposition to removal, as the Cherokees were offended and angered by suggestions that their failure to support the minority-made Treaty of New Echota reflected merely the bitter fruit of faction politics rather than a serious complaint against an illegitimate compact. A British visitor who witnessed the meeting, George Featherstonhaugh, left with far more sympathy for the Cherokees than the U.S. government. He later reported on what he witnessed in his memoir *A Canoe Voyage up the Minnay Sotor*, and in the process offered a succinct sketch of the removal issue as a whole:

> A whole Indian nation abandons the pagan practices of their ancestors, adopts the Christian religion, uses books printed in their own language, submits to the government of their elders, builds houses and temples of worship, relies upon agriculture

for their support, and produces men of great ability to rule over them.... Are not these the great principles of civilization? They were driven from their religious and social state then, not because they cannot be civilized, but because a pseudo set of civilized beings, who are too strong for them want their possessions![2]

In early 1838, John Ross and a delegation of other Cherokee leaders, including Elijah Hicks and Whitepath, traveled again to Washington, D.C. They brought with them the signatures of 15,665 Cherokees protesting the Treaty of New Echota. The Commissioner of Indian Affairs told them that the Senate Committee on Indian Affairs had met and voted to sanction the president's plans to carry out the treaty. Outraged citizens from around the United States sent messages and petitions on behalf of the Cherokee cause. Nonetheless, Van Buren ordered that seven thousand soldiers be assembled to prepare for action. Time had run out. On May 23, 1838, the military roundup of the Cherokee Nation began.

Removal

Replacing John Wool as the military commander of the removal campaign was Major General Winfield Scott, known as "Old Fuss and Feathers," a veteran of the War of 1812, the Blackhawk War, the Seminole Wars, and at one time nearly a duelist against Andrew Jackson. Scott looked at his mission without enthusiasm; when he realized that many of the Georgia troops seemed as interested in killing the Cherokees as removing them, he realized the extent of the challenge he faced. He attempted to bring order to a chaotic situation.

His address to the Cherokees offered equal parts warning and plea:

Chiefs, head-men and warriors! Will you then, by resistance, compel us to resort to arms? God forbid! Or will you, by flight, seek to hid yourselves in mountains and forests, and thus oblige us to hunt you down? Remember that, in pursuit, it may be impossible to avoid conflicts. The blood of the white man or the blood of the red man may be spilt, and, if spilt, however accidentally, it may be impossible for the discreet and humane among you, or among us, to prevent a general war and carnage. Think of this, my Cherokee brethren! I am an old warrior, and have been present at many a scene of slaughter, but spare me, I beseech you, the horror of witnessing the destruction of the Cherokees.[3]

Within four weeks in May and June, separate military operations in Georgia, Tennessee, North Carolina, and Alabama succeeded in removing roughly seventeen thousand Cherokees from their homes at gunpoint and gathering them together in various containment camps that had been constructed for the purpose of Cherokee prisoners. It soon became clear that the preparations made for the event were not satisfactory. In general the camps were hardly more than fenced pens, with little shelter from the elements and no arrangements for basic sanitation. The hardships these living arrangements created were exacerbated by the fact that the roundups were conducted as surprise operations, parting husband from wife and parents from children, so that some Cherokees had nothing but the clothes on their backs, and many possessed only what they could carry.

John G. Burnett, a soldier involved with the roundup, described the operation:

> Men working in the fields were arrested and driven to the stockades. Women were dragged from their homes by soldiers whose language they could not understand. Children were often separated from their parents and driven into the stockades with the sky for a blanket and the earth for a pillow.... In another home was a frail Mother, apparently a widow and three small children, one just a baby. When told that she must go the Mother gathered the children at her feet, prayed an humble prayer in her native tongue, patted the old family dog on the head, told the faithful creature good-by, with a baby strapped on her back and leading a child with each hand started on her exile. But the task was too great for the frail Mother. A stroke of heart failure relieved her suffering. She sunk and died with her baby on her back, and her other two children clinging to her hands.[4]

One Georgia volunteer, who became a Confederate Colonel during the Civil War, later admitted to ethnographer James Mooney, "I fought through the civil war and have seen men shot to pieces and slaughtered by thousands, but the Cherokee removal was the cruelest work I ever knew."[5]

To make matters worse, a terrible drought struck the Southeast at almost the same time the roundup began. Without adequate supplies or facilities, the camps became breeding grounds for dysentery and other diseases, and the dangerous heat added to the unhealthy mix. As with the rest of removal, the young and the elderly suffered most. Various scholars have speculated that the camp conditions might have been responsible for perhaps one-third to one-half of all of the deaths associated with the Trail of Tears, though the records leave little chance for anything more than speculation.

Scott divided the camps into three military districts, each with its own plan for removal to Indian Territory involving land and water routes. Two groups were stationed along the Tennessee River, one at Ross's Landing (at present-day Chattanooga, Tennessee) and one at Gunter's Landing (at Guntersville, Alabama). The third group went to the Cherokee Agency on the Hiwassee River (at Calhoun, Tennessee). From each of these starting points, groups were to be dispatched to make the trek to Indian Country through a combination of land and water passages by foot and by boat. As none of the passages was direct, the distance of the trek averaged approximately 1,200 miles. The first three groups faced disastrous conditions with heat and sickness, and more died.

Despite Scott's attempts to watch the Georgia troops in particular, and to exhort all of the soldiers to treat the Cherokees in a humane manner, his best intentions were not entirely successful. Baptist missionary Evan Jones, a white man who lived and worked among the Cherokees and shared their fate when they were removed West, wrote of their experience in July 1838: "The work of war in a time of peace, is commenced in the Georgia part of the Cherokee Nation, and is carried on, in most cases, in the most unfeeling and brutal manner; no regard being paid to the orders of the commanding General, in regard to humane treatment of the Indians."[6]

Defeated in his attempts to thwart removal, John Ross appealed to General Scott for delays until the weather cooled, and also asked that the remainder of the relocation logistics be turned over to the Cherokee Council, which had a greater vested interest in the Cherokees surviving their journey. General Scott agreed. Thereafter, John Ross himself became the architect of the removal process he had fought for so long.

The Cherokee-organized marches started on August 28, 1838. Thirteen groups of roughly a thousand each slowly made their way west. John Ross, carrying the laws and records of the Cherokee Nation, left with the last group of sick and infirm Cherokees in December. Thousands were trapped by the harsh winter conditions before they could cross the Mississippi River, and once again, many died. Ross's own wife succumbed to illness on the trail on February 1, 1839; like so many others, she was buried in a shallow grave in the little time that could be spared before the Cherokees again had to march. The last party did not reach its destination until late March.

Determining the cost of the Trail of Tears in human lives is a difficult proposition. In the first wave of relocation, soldiers had strong motivation to underreport deaths. (The original official number provided by the government was approximately four hundred.) When the Cherokees themselves had some control over the removal process, they were more concerned about keeping each other alive than with documenting each loss along the way, even if they had possessed the means. Traditional approximations suggest that some four thousand Cherokees died of hunger, exposure, dysentery, whooping cough, violence, and other factors during or because of the Trail of Tears. This figure may date from one single missionary's 1839 estimation, repeated and cited until it gained the credibility of fact; at any rate, recent scholarship suggests that the death toll figure of four thousand may represent only half of the actual Cherokee lives lost.[7] Regardless of the exact statistics, though, removal exacted a terrible toll on the people of the Cherokee Nation.

In 1968, the National Historic Trails System Act established the National Historic Trails System in the United States in order to commemorate important national routes and promote their preservation. In 1987, Congress designated the Trail of Tears National Historic Trail, which covers approximately 2,200 miles of land and water routes, intersecting nine different states. The Trail of Tears Trail refers specifically to those paths taken on the removal of the Cherokee Nation in 1838 and 1839. In 1993, the National Park Service partnered with the newly formed Trail of Tears Association to promote awareness about the trail and oversee its management and development.

Slaves

If determining the number of Cherokee dead is difficult, then it is even more challenging to reconstruct the experiences of the black slaves who were forced to travel the Trail of Tears with their Cherokee owners. As many as two thousand slaves may have been removed along with the Cherokee Nation. Members of the Cherokee economic elite had adopted the Southern plantation system, along with slavery, from the English colonials before the United States was formed. While the practice was not widespread among average Cherokee households, it remained among some of the wealthiest families.

Some slave-owning Cherokees shifted their households to Indian Territory in the two years between the Treaty of New Echota and the forced removal campaign. Major Ridge was one of these.

Such relocations, while not of their own choosing, were at least more comfortable for all concerned than the deadly marches that followed. Other slaves shared the fate of their owners and suffered through the Trail of Tears. John Ross, for example, was not only the final coordinator of removal, but also a slaveowner who moved his family and household during some of the most treacherous of conditions.

Although the Cherokees had watched firsthand as the U.S. system failed them, most chose to renew their commitment to certain institutions inspired by the United States and its colonial predecessors once they reached Indian Territory. One of these was slavery, and another was the constitution, which enforced this practice. The close of the U.S. Civil War brought an end to slavery in the Cherokee Nation. And the legacy of Cherokee slaveholding, as well as the Trail of Tears, continues to be felt in the twenty-first century, as the descendants of freedmen—who spoke the Cherokee language, lived among the Cherokee people, suffered the Trail of Tears along with their owners, and shared their exile in Indian Territory—sue the Cherokee Nation of Oklahoma to become Cherokee citizens. The controversy hinges on the issue of blood. Cherokee law denies citizenship to those without Cherokee blood, but the descendants of the freedmen claim that by culture and by right, they have earned a place in the nation.[8]

Tsali

While all of the Cherokees were, in one form or another, victims of the Trail of Tears, not all were removed to Indian Territory. In North Carolina, for example, one group had separated from the Cherokee Nation and lived in an area known as Quallatown, where they were led by Chief Drowning Bear and his advisor, William Holland Thomas, a white merchant who had been adopted and raised by the Cherokees. Thomas acted as a liaison between the Cherokees and the U.S. government, arguing that the Quallatown Cherokees were either North Carolina citizens or qualified and willing to become such, and therefore did not fall under the Treaty of New Echota. Thomas ultimately succeeded in negotiating safety for the Quallatown Cherokees. In return, however, he pledged to General Winfield Scott that this group would not harbor other Cherokees who sought to elude U.S. forces. This left the Quallatown Cherokees in the position of either watching their fellow Cherokees be hunted down, or helping the enemy forces who were doing the hunting.

There were also Cherokees who fled from U.S. troops and sought to hide in the Smoky Mountains. Their story is the one immortalized in the contemporary Cherokee, North Carolina, drama "Unto These Hills," and the tale of their escape from removal has taken on a near-mythic quality. The traditional account of these fugitives and their martyr-savior, Tsali, was captured by early ethnologist James Mooney in his landmark book *Myths of the Cherokees.* He compiled the tale from interviews given by Tsali's surviving son, an elderly William Holland Thomas, and other Cherokees:

> One old man named Tsali, "Charley," was seized with his wife, his brother, his three sons and their families. Exasperated at the brutality accorded his wife, who, being unable to travel fast, was prodded with bayonets to hasten her steps, he urged the other men to join with him in a dash for liberty. As he spoke in Cherokee the soldiers, although they heard, understood nothing until each warrior suddenly sprang upon the one nearest and endeavored to wrench his gun from him. The attack was so sudden and unexpected that one soldier was killed and the rest fled, while the Indians escaped to the mountains. Hundreds of others, some of them from the various stockades, managed also to escape to the mountains from time to time, where those who did not die of starvation subsisted on roots and wild berries until the hunt was over. Finding it impracticable to secure these fugitives, General Scott finally tendered them a proposition, through (Colonel) W. R. Thomas, their most trusted friend, that if they would surrender Charley and his party for punishment, the rest would be allowed to remain until their case could be adjusted by the government. On hearing of the proposition, Charley voluntarily came in with his sons, offering himself as a sacrifice for his people. By command of General Scott, Charley, his brother, and the two elder sons were shot near the mouth of the Tuckasegee, a detachment of Cherokee prisoners being compelled to do the shooting in order to impress upon the Indians the fact of their utter helplessness. From those fugitives thus permitted to remain originated the eastern band of Cherokee.[9]

Many of the details of the Tsali story are not easily verifiable. The Quallatown Cherokees, to protect their own agreement with the United States, seem to have helped find Tsali. The facts of the original killings, and of any negotiations made by Tsali, are unclear. However, official reports to Winfield Scott do note that Tsali and members of his family were executed in November 1838; moreover, Colonel William S. Foster, whose duty it was to find those responsible for the deaths of the soldiers, did recommend that the other refugees be allowed to remain in North Carolina. Approximately 1,400

Cherokees did not make the trek West. Of those, more than a thousand were in North Carolina. Less acculturated than many of the other Cherokees, this group tended to include fullblood purists who preferred to practice a traditional Cherokee lifestyle rather than assimilate with U.S. society. This remnant of the Cherokee Nation formed what is now the Eastern band of Cherokees.

The Cherokee Rose

The story of Tsali has a legendary quality about it, but other stories from the Trail of Tears take myth a step further, while making meaningful commentary about the nature of U.S. Indian removal. One such story is the legend of the Cherokee rose. Widely available now on everything from postcards to calendars, the tale is a simple one. As the soldiers forced the Cherokees to march West, the Cherokee mothers wept for their dying children. The elders prayed that some reassuring sign would appear to give them strength. After these prayers were said, flowers grew from each spot where a Cherokee mother's tear hit the ground. The story ascribes significance to each aspect of the flower—the white color represents the mothers' tears; the gold centers represent the gold taken from Cherokee national lands; and the seven petals represent the seven clans of the Cherokee Nation—and to the fact that it grows naturally in the areas through which the trail routes passed.

Although this story is not properly termed history, it is significant because it captures a certain persistent memory about the Trail of Tears experience, and its power in the public consciousness. In 1916, the Cherokee rose became the state flower of Georgia.

Notes

1. Quoted in Grant Foreman, *Indian Removal: The Emigration of the Five Civilized Tribes of Indians* (Norman: University of Oklahoma Press, 1972), pp. 271, 272.

2. Quoted in Grace Steele Woodward, *The Cherokees* (Norman: University of Oklahoma Press, 1963), p. 197.

3. Quoted in *A Wilderness Still the Cradle of Nature: Frontier Georgia*, ed. Edward J. Cashin (Savannah, GA: Beehive Press, 1994), pp. 137–138.

4. John G. Burnett, "The Cherokee Removal Through the Eyes of a Private Soldier," *Journal of Cherokee Studies* 3 (1978):180–185, 183.

5. James Mooney, *Historical Sketch of the Cherokee* (reprint, Chicago: Aldine, 1975), p. 124.

6. Evan Jones, "Letters," in *The Cherokee Removal: A Brief History with Documents*, ed. Theda Perdue and Michael D. Green, 2nd ed. (New York: Bedford/St. Martin's, 2005), pp. 171–176, 173.

7. See Russell Thornton, "The Demography of the Trail of Tears Period: A New Estimate of Cherokee Population Losses," in *Cherokee Removal: Before and After*, ed. William J. Anderson (Athens: University of Georgia Press, 1991), pp. 75–95.

8. Claudio Saunt, "Jim Crow and the Indians," *Salon.com*, February 21, 2006, available at http://www.salon.com/news/feature/2006/02/21/cherokee/index_np.html (accessed February 21, 2006); and S. E. Ruckman, "Freedman's Status Remains in Limbo: Cherokees Mull Vote on Enrollment," *Tulsa World*, May 1, 2006, p. A16.

9. James Mooney, "The Story of Tsali, as Related to James Mooney by the Cherokees," in *Voices from the Trail of Tears*, ed. Vicki Rozema (Winston-Salem, NC: John F. Blair, 2003), pp. 157–158.

CHAPTER 6

AFTERMATH

In the United States

With the dispossession of the Cherokee Nation via the Trail of Tears, the previous relocations of the Choctaw, Creek, and Chickasaw Nations, and the defeat and ejection of the Seminole Nation, new U.S. policy toward Native America was established. If U.S. forces could confiscate the property and remove the members of the so-called "Five Civilized Tribes," the groups with whom U.S. citizens seemed to share the closest relationship, then the same action could be taken against other native nations, ones that seemed more foreign and less sympathetic to whites. From such policies came the reservation system, the practice of assigning native peoples to specified federal lands (such as those in "Indian Territory"), and the trust system, the practice of the U.S. government holding funds owed to native nations on their behalf, much in the same way as guardians would hold property on behalf of their wards.

Removal remained the principal U.S. strategy for native peoples, and other nations suffered the same fate as the Cherokees had in their deadly march. Perhaps the most infamous of the later removals was the Long March of the Navajo in 1863–1864. The United States met significant resistance from Western Native Americans, however, and the rest of the nineteenth century became known for costly and violent "Indian Wars" with nations such as the Apache, the Nez Perce, and the Sioux.

Despite the fact that a few notable individuals responded publicly to the removal issue either in favor of the policy or in protest against it, the Trail of Tears was not a truly significant event in the lives of most U.S. citizens—or even their elected leaders. Removal had been a favorite issue of Andrew Jackson, but he was no longer in office, and President Martin Van Buren's time and attention were centered primarily on the country's financial depression. In the election of 1840, Van Buren lost the White House to "Old Tippeca-noe," William Henry Harrison. Although he styled himself much as Andrew Jackson had, as a "log cabin" everyman and Indian fighter, he had little chance to make an impact on U.S. policy of any kind; he died only a month after his inauguration.

His vice president, John Tyler, assumed executive office during a time that was rife not only with economic concerns, but also with sectional disputes. The question of expansion—exacerbated by specific challenges in the cases of Texas, California, and New Mexico—brought with it increased tensions between the Northern and Southern states. Slavery was the primary subject of contention. U.S. policy toward Native America followed in the direction it had begun under Jackson, but Tyler, like Van Buren, found other subjects of more immediate concern.

Interestingly enough, some of the important figures in the debate over slavery were leaders of "Jacksonian" reform movements, the same people who had protested U.S. treatment of the Cherokee Nation during removal. These individuals and the reform groups they represented supported abolition, the ending of slavery and freeing of slaves, for the same reasons they had argued for justice and human rights for the Cher-okees. Ultimately, the abolitionists' arguments against the institution of slavery met more success than previous defenses of the Cherokees had. It took a violent civil war for the issue to be resolved, however.

In Indian Territory

The Trail of Tears had more immediate and extreme implica-tions for the Cherokee Nation. The assassinations of the Treaty Party leadership left Principal Chief John Ross alone to come to terms with the tragic aftermath of forced removal. One of his greatest challenges was to face the Cherokees who had settled Indian Territory long before the recent exodus. The Old Settlers, as they called themselves, included cultural purists, such as Sequoyah, who had willingly cho-sen exile from their homeland over assimilation with U.S. ways. An 1810 Cherokee law made these Cherokees expatriates, a people with-out a nation. But when Ross and his citizens came to Indian Terri-tory, they brought the Cherokee Nation with them. The expatriates found themselves surrounded by the tattered remnants of the body politic they had fled. The defiant Old Settlers and the exhausted émigrés found themselves revisiting an old debate once again.

In his 1965 work *The Colonizer and the Colonized*, Tunisian phi-losopher Albert Memmi suggests a model for analyzing the cultural clash between an indigenous population and a colonial power. First, he notes, the native peoples observe the power structure that the colonists impose. When they realize that only the colonizers gain in this system, they seek to emulate it: "There is a tempting model very close at hand—the colonizer. The latter suffers none of his deficiencies, has all rights, enjoys every possession, and benefits from every prestige.... The first ambition of the colonized is to become equal to that splendid model and to resemble him to the point of disappearing in him."[1]

Prior to 1839, however, the Cherokee experience failed to follow Memmi's model convincingly. Although the majority of the people of the Cherokee Nation eventually committed to assimilation, they refused the ultimate invitation to enjoy "rights," "possession," and "benefits"—they declined Thomas Jefferson's offer of complete U.S. citizenship and the protection that would follow, at the expense of Cherokee identity. Instead, they followed the campaign of simultaneous acculturation and separation that left them especially vulnerable to Jacksonian policy.

Memmi's analysis did not end there. When such a violent event as forced removal ends all hopes of fair treatment and successful integration, Memmi argues that native peoples respond with a cultural backlash. They return to old ways and embrace tradition. In Memmi's words,

> He has been haughtily shown that he could never assimilate with others; he has been scornfully thrown back toward what is in him which could not be assimilated by others. Very well, then! He is, he shall be, that man. The same passion which made him absorb Europe shall make him assert his differences; since those differences, after all, are within him and correctly constitute his true self.[2]

In 1839, then, according to Memmi, the Cherokees should have harnessed their collective grief and disillusionment and outrage with the U.S. republic they had mirrored and used that momentum to fuel a purist movement of extreme proportions.

They did not. In the darkest hour of the Cherokee Nation, the Old Settlers and New Settlers reached agreement and, together, they ratified a national constitution. In its pages they reaffirmed the nation's faith in a constitutional republic, and pledged themselves anew to the goals of the Jeffersonian civilization campaign. Of Andrew Jackson, the man who called himself the new Jefferson, and John Ross, the principal chief of the Cherokees, it seems that the latter remained the more Jeffersonian. Interestingly enough, by dedicating himself to the causes of consensus, the rule of law, and political debate, Ross also acted as a traditional Cherokee.

When the survivors of forced removal arrived in Indian Territory, they found the Old Settlers living modest lives primarily as subsistence farmers, and also as local traders and operators of gristmills and saltworks. Sequoyah ran a school and taught the Cherokee syllabary but little interest in education reached beyond that. Uniform law and law enforcement took a decentralized, locally driven form. These exiles shared a vision of the past—or, perhaps more accurately, a distaste for one particular vision of the future—and so together they tried to simply survive. Life was, to use Woodward's words, "casual, informal, and rustic."[3] That life left only a tenuous welcome for the influx of emigrants from the so-called Trail of Tears.

The divisions between the Old Settlers and the Trail of Tears survivors—the divisions that had helped to persuade the Western Cherokees to leave their homeland in the first place—consisted of more than a simple disagreement over lifestyles. The purism of the Old Settlers did not merely reflect the desire to return to subsistence farming or the monolingual dependence on the Cherokee language. This purism had political dimensions. These Cherokees favored a decentralized, locally based government like the traditional Cherokee town council/clan system. The system they had instituted in Indian Territory reflected this perspective.

The Old Settlers made the first move when their chiefs sent a combined invitation to the Cherokee Nation leadership to meet at Double Springs in June of 1839 and officially accept the Old Settlers' hand of friendship. Less than a week into that meeting of welcome, the Old Settler chiefs asked Ross to commit his views on the future of Cherokee government to paper for their consideration. In the resulting resolutions Ross distinguished between the "Western Cherokees" (the Old Settlers) and the "Eastern Cherokees" (those forcibly removed on the Trail of Tears). He suggested that three current leaders from each group—specifically, John Brown, John Looney, and John Rogers from the Western Cherokees and George Lowrey, Edward Gunter, and Ross himself—as well as three more Cherokees elected from each side for this purpose join together as a committee with the intent of revising and drafting a code of laws for the government of the Cherokee Nation "with the hope that it may also be adopted by the representatives of the Western Cherokees."[4] Ross and the New Settlers, then, assumed that the issue revolved around modifying the Cherokee Nation's previous government to satisfy the Old Settlers.

Western Cherokee Chief John Brown disagreed. He answered that by accepting the Old Settlers' hand of friendship both symbolically and literally—the settled Cherokees had provided a great deal of assistance to the survivors of removal—the Eastern Cherokees had agreed to live as Western Cherokees. This included respecting Western Cherokee government, such as it was. According to Brown, the Cherokee Nation proper had disappeared. Brown and his fellow chiefs then dissolved the meeting with Ross and the others, leaving them to contemplate the idea that their government and their positions might suddenly have ceased to exist. Ross was unprepared for this Old Settler position and greatly concerned about what it meant for the Eastern Cherokees: "they [the Old Settlers] require the unconditional submission of the whole body of the people who have lately arrived, to laws and regulations in the making of which they have had no voice. The attempt of a small minority to enforce their will over a great majority, contrary to their wishes, appears to us ... repugnant to reason."[5]

The mediator that emerged between the Western and the Eastern Cherokees salvaged the June summit between Old Settlers and New Settlers despite his own ambiguous vision of Cherokee civilization. Sequoyah once again assumed a key role for his people. As a revered figure from both sides, Sequoyah had the name recognition with the Easterners and the credibility with the Westerners to arbitrate between them. With his help the two sides agreed to convene a council to form a new government. The intention seemed clear; they would revise neither group's preexisting system. They would create something new.

In July, Western Chief George Lowrey and spokesman Sequoyah presided over the conference at the Illinois Park Ground. The meeting drew interested Cherokees as well as elected leadership such as John Ross and Eastern Chief John Looney. Urging even more to attend, Sequoyah wrote: "We, the old settlers, are here in council with the late emigrants and we want you to come up without delay, that we may talk matters over like friends and brothers. These people are here in great multitudes, and they are perfectly friendly towards us." Solemn debates took place as the park ground transformed into a large-scale town council with mass participation. Sequoyah noted that all seemed to recognize the import of the sober deliberations: "there are upwards of two thousand people on the ground.... we have no doubt but we can have all things amicably and satisfactorily settled."[6] Despite the recent trend toward governmental centralization in the East and the disheartening exile in the West, both sides rekindled the Cherokee love for political debate. The numbers grew.

The Illinois Park Ground conference yielded The Act of Union on July 12, 1839. This act joined the Old Settlers and the Trail of Tears survivors into "'one body politic'" known by "the title of the Cherokee nation." It also set in motion the election of a national assembly composed of Eastern and Western Cherokees and set the site of the new capital of the nation, the centrally located town of Tahlequah, where it remains to this day.

Despite attention to issues of representation and parity, nothing could change the fact that the Eastern Cherokees outnumbered the Old Settlers significantly. (Historian Grace Steele Woodward figures that the recent Trail of Tears survivors accounted for fully four-fifths of the Cherokees in Indian Territory.)[7] It came as no surprise, then, when the new mixed assembly elected John Ross, even more popular among the Trail of Tears survivors after his handling of removal, as the first principal chief of the new Cherokee Nation. Western Cherokee David Vann, however, became assistant principal chief, the second highest position in the nation. The mixed assembly with its mixed leadership undertook the drafting of a new constitution.

This would not be the first constitution of the Cherokee Nation. The nation had written and ratified a compact in 1827 which had served them until the state of Georgia declared it null and void and U.S. President Andrew Jackson acquiesced. The national assembly in 1839 agreed to use this previous, pre-removal constitution as the template for the new compact. Within a month, the assembly quickly wrote and ratified the constitution. Its main departure from the 1827 compact came in the election of the principal and assistant principal chiefs. In the earlier compact, the legislature voted for these positions. In the 1839 constitution, the people elected them directly. Concern for legitimacy, particularly in this delicate time between the Old and New Settlers, led to this change. On September 6, 1839, the president of the National Convention, George Lowrey, signed the document and pronounced it law. New elections followed. Once again both Old and New Settlers found representation, and once again the people elected John Ross and David Vann as principal chief and assistant principal chief, respectively. Old Settlers gained fully one-third of the positions. Ross speculated that the Eastern Cherokees would vote for respected Western Cherokee leaders, in many cases, as gestures of good will, because of "the anxiety which exists to restore peace and quietude throughout the Country."[8]

Even though a vocal cultural purist minority took part in the convention, the constitution of 1839, like the 1827 compact it followed, reflected a conscious emulation of the U.S. system. In the articles and sections of the constitution the Cherokee framers provided for a separation of powers between the executive, legislative, and judicial branches of the government with checks and balances between them. The Cherokees provided for a bicameral legislature like the U.S. Congress. A ten-point article like the U.S. Bill of Rights ended the document. The framers—namely William Shorey Coodey, the man primarily responsible for writing the considered draft of the document—also lifted many phrases and lines directly from the U.S. Constitution.

Only a few key differences separated the Cherokee constitution from the U.S. one. First, the Cherokees made allowances for the unique status of their post-removal territory granted by the U.S. federal government. The Cherokees would hold their land in Indian Territory in common; they considered improvements on the land, however, like any other private property and provided that they be protected as such. Second, the 1839 document copied the 1827 constitution's restriction against black political participation. This did not reflect simple anti-non-Cherokee sentiment. The framers allowed full rights for the mixed-blood children of unions with all other non-Cherokee peoples—members of other indigenous nations, whites, Spanish peoples, etc.—as long as they lived within Cherokee national borders and maintained their Cherokee citizenship. The constitution hindered only slaves, free blacks, or the mulatto descendants of them, any "person who is negro and mulatto parentage" (Article III, Section 5).[9]

Third, the Cherokees included a religious element not found in the U.S. Constitution. All would-be officeholders had to pass a religious test to ensure that "no person who denies the being of a God or future state of reward and punishment, shall hold any office." The framers also added direct statements of faith, "acknowledging, with humility and gratitude, the goodness of the Sovereign Ruler of the Universe ... and imploring His aid and guidance" (Preamble). In the freedom of religion section, they deviated from the U.S. Constitution's words and expanded the clause to read "The free exercise of religious worship, and serving God without distinction, shall forever be enjoyed" (Article V, Section 1).

The differences between the Cherokee National Constitution and the U.S. Constitution were intentional. The issue of land ownership seems self-explanatory; the Cherokees had held lands—specific, defined, finite lands—in common in the past, and recognized individual property rights to all improvements. This became especially convenient again in Indian Territory because the U.S. federal government tended to treat the Cherokees' land rights as common anyway, at least prior to the Dawes Act of 1887.

The constitutional issue of race, or, more accurately, the Cherokee concern with the black race, stems from several sources. Obviously, the Cherokees sought to capture and preserve one particular view of racial rank, one that did not place them at the bottom of the hierarchy, one that actually gave them control over another race. The 1827 constitution in fact confirmed the Cherokee position about the racial spectrum. It also suggests a Cherokee desire to institutionalize the emerging plantation-slavery worldview of the nineteenth century, another nod to Jefferson's civilization campaign and its many corresponding forms of assimilation.

By the time of the 1839 constitution, the Cherokees did not need to prove their degree of acculturation by overtly embracing a system of racial dominance. Perhaps, then, the need came from more internal sources. It is true that slavery remained in Indian Territory. John Ross, for example, brought his slaves with him during removal. But slavery no longer played the economic role it once had. Indeed, the Cherokee economy, like so many Cherokees themselves, died on the so-called Trail of Tears.

Perhaps by preserving the racial component of the 1827 constitution, the Cherokee framers intended to reassure themselves about their place in the world. The recent Trail of Tears survivors had experienced a violent uprooting and coerced relocation. It had to be difficult to consider themselves a people above others and apart from them while enduring a cross-country forced march. Retaining racial distinctions reminded them that, despite their misfortune, others still fared worse by failing to be born Cherokee. Excluding blacks, then, remained one of the last means available to them to assert (or reclaim) their corporate feelings of superiority and power.

The religious aspects of the Cherokee Constitution spoke to the widespread Christianization of the Cherokees by the mid-nineteenth century. Although at first reluctant to accept Christianity, the Cherokees eventually converted in mass numbers in a short amount of time, largely because of mission schools and specific missionaries who worked in them. Despite their traditional ways, many of the Old Settlers accepted Christianity, some even before their journey west. The issue of religion, then, represented an area of consensus between both groups. Samuel Worcester exemplified the importance of missionaries as political as well as spiritual figures. His work with the Cherokees gained particular visibility with his steady publication in *The Cherokee Phoenix*, usually on anthropological subjects, and his role in *Worcester v. Georgia*, as a legal advocate for the Cherokees. He relocated with the Cherokees and continued his work with them after removal.

Missionaries such as Worcester blended religious teaching with political activism. Their converts, it seems, did the same.

Beyond simply espousing a broad monotheistic faith, the Cherokee framers seemed anxious to preserve a certain moral order on the Indian Territory frontier. The Preamble provides an immediate reminder of the Cherokees' debt to "the Sovereign Ruler of the Universe," and the religious test assured that no official would fail to believe in "Him." The freedom of religion section placed limits on Cherokees' liberty: "provided, that this liberty of conscience shall not be construed as to excuse acts of licentiousness, or justify practices inconsistent with the peace or safety of this nation" (Article V, Section 2). It seems the framers hoped that a document infused with the language of faith might capture and preserve the moral fortitude necessary to help the Cherokees rebuild their world again.

Despite these differences, however, the Cherokee Constitution of 1839 clearly reflected the organization, content, and language of the U.S. Constitution. On the one hand, this similarity proves that the Eastern Cherokees, the survivors of forced removal, won control over the Cherokee Nation's political structure. The same Cherokees, after all, had ratified the template for the 1839 constitution in 1827. These Cherokees had embraced and largely achieved the goals of Jefferson's civilization campaign. These Cherokees had, to use Mary Young's phrase, mirrored the U.S. republic.

But the ratification of the constitution also represented a new consensus, or at least the beginnings of a new consensus, between the Old Settlers and the Eastern Cherokees. The Western Cherokees accepted positions under the new constitution and shared power with their émigré cousins. Although violent disagreements would flare between the factions until after the U.S. Civil War, the constitution of 1839 would survive the strife and eventually unite all parties. Strife came not only from purist/assimilationist disagreements between the Old Settlers and New Settlers, but also from the periphery, from the followers of the assassinated Treaty Party leadership. In particular, Stand Watie, younger brother of Elias Boudinot, repeatedly challenged Ross and the Cherokee national government. Watie went so far as to appeal to U.S. President Van Buren to seek U.S. military aid in bringing his brother's assassins (whom he believed to be Ross and the National Party leadership) to justice. In the end, however, the document reaffirmed and maintained a Cherokee decision to recognize the United States as the best model for Cherokee society, despite the recent Cherokee experience of the Trail of Tears.

Memmi's model for indigenous behavior makes intuitive sense. If a native population tried to emulate its colonizer's system, and that colonizer still dismissed and denied the people, surely the natives would rebel against the colonizer and the system both. The Cherokees experienced this rebuke and denial in a twofold manner. First, their successes failed to bring them acceptance as a civilization. Georgians declared their laws invalid and their property forfeit. Despite the Cherokees' accomplishments, they could not garner respect from the states. Second, the Cherokees watched the system they imitated utterly fail. Although the U.S. Supreme Court found in favor of the Cherokees, the executive ignored the legislature and imposed illegal policy. If Georgia's disregard for the Cherokee Nation did not shake the Cherokees' faith, then surely Jackson's disregard for the U.S. government should have. Yet, after witnessing this failure on the part of the U.S. system, and experiencing the Trail of Tears, the Cherokees adopted a structure similar to the United States within months of arriving in Indian Territory.

In short, the Eastern Cherokees still believed in the system that had failed them. They blamed individuals rather than the process. When John Ross addressed the new Cherokee National Assembly on September 12, 1839, he advised its members to wait until the U.S. system corrected itself and gave the Cherokees the justice owed to them:

> Friends and Fellow Citizens, by the provisions of the Constitution which has been adopted in pursuance of the Act uniting the Eastern and Western Cherokee Nation into one Body politic, you have been elected to fill the Seats you occupy. And by the free suffrage of the people, it has become my duty to submit for your deliberation and action, such subjects, as in my judgment for the public good seem to require.... Our friendly relations with the Govt. and Citizens of the United States, should be firmly maintained. And for all past injuries, which we have individually and collectively sustained, either in person or property, from the unjust and illegal acts of the State or U. States Govt. or from the citizens thereof—we should peaceably seek, and patiently await redress from the scales of justice upheld by the arm of the United States.[10]

Ross's faith in "the scales of justice upheld by the arm of the United States"—the Eastern Cherokees' faith in their own similar constitution—reveals the degree to which the Cherokee identity now rested upon Euro-U.S. foundations. But those foundations survived only because they rested on even earlier and more ancient ones: the Cherokee emphasis on consensus, the rule of law, open debate, and civic participation. Or, to turn phrases in on themselves, the Cherokees followed the U.S. model because it was so Cherokee.

The constitution of 1839 did not solve the problems of the Cherokee Nation. It did, however, survive them. Under this compact the Cherokee Nation, an ambiguous blend of the traditional and the assimilated, reknit after the Trail of Tears, endured for nearly 140 years.

Notes

1. Albert Memmi, *The Colonizer and the Colonized*, trans. Howard Greenfeld (Boston: Beacon Press, 1965), p. 120.

2. Ibid., p. 132.

3. Grace Steele Woodward, *The Cherokees* (Norman: University of Oklahoma Press, 1963), p. 223.

4. John Ross to John Brown, John Looney, and John Rogers, June 13, 1839, in *The Papers of Chief John Ross*, vol. 1, ed. Gary E. Moulton (Norman: University of Oklahoma Press, 1985), p. 714.

5. John Ross to Montfort Stokes, June 21, 1839, in *The Papers of Chief John Ross*, vol. 1, p. 715.

6. Quoted in Grant Foreman, *The Five Civilized Tribes* (Norman: University of Oklahoma Press, 1932), p. 299.

7. Woodward, *The Cherokees*, p. 222.

8. John Ross to Matthew Arbuckle, September 5, 1839, in *The Papers of Chief John Ross*, vol. 1, p. 760.

9. "The 1839 Cherokee Constitution," available at http://www.cherokeeobserver.org/Issues/1839constitution.html (accessed October 12, 2005). See the Primary Documents section.

10. John Ross, "Address to the National Council," September 12, 1839, in *The Papers of Chief John Ross*, vol. 1, p. 761.

EPILOGUE

For the world, the Trail of Tears offered another example of an ongoing pattern of force, the tendency, to once again borrow the United Nations' definition of ethnic cleansing, for the powerful to use their might to relocate those who are different from them and take their victims' property, often using nationalistic language to describe and defend the theft they have perpetrated. Being counted among the number of nations who have followed this tradition is no honor. And the fact that the terminology did not exist in that era does not excuse the guilty. Those who protested Cherokee removal recognized its faults despite the fact that they did not name it ethnic cleansing. Clearly Ralph Waldo Emerson recognized wrongdoing when he warned President Martin Van Buren, "However feeble the sufferer and however great the oppressor, it is in the nature of things that the blow should recoil upon the aggressor."[1]

Ironically, at the same time Indian removal became standard policy (following the world pattern of ethnic cleansing), many in the United States created a myth of exceptionalism for their nation, claiming that the country was different from all others because of its Manifest Destiny—because of its frontier. Of course, the land was not frontier until its tenants had been relocated. But, in circular fashion, the argument went that removal was necessary so that the frontier would exist and could be settled. So went the Apaches when newly annexed Texas called for the national government to remove no less than 25,000; so went the Navajo on the Long Walk; so fled the Nez Perce from the Idaho canyons. Barely five years after the Trail of Tears, only very few Native Americans still remained east of the Mississippi River. By the end of the century, the long arm of the East had expanded fully West across the United States, scattering the native nations, continuing the pattern.

As it did so, the United States also continued its shift from Jeffersonianism to Jacksonianism, with its paradoxical emphasis on expanding the franchise while at the same time concentrating and centralizing power. From such fields grew more vibrant nationalism, even imperialism. Manifest Destiny eventually spilled over the continent's borders to pertain to farther shores, in both metaphorical and tangible ways. Meanwhile, the U.S. Army turned its face inward, fighting America's native nations, finishing the process the Trail of Tears had begun.

The story of the Trail of Tears is an epic one of colliding cultures and overwhelming forces, but it also is instructive in the way it underscores individuals, caught in unique moments in time, and all of the richness and complexity of their motivations and loyalties. Andrew Jackson threatened war when South Carolinians tried to nullify a law, but he turned into a states'-rights advocate when Georgians nullified an entire nation. Major Ridge had once killed to enforce the very law he broke by signing the Treaty of New Echota. Samuel Worcester chose imprisonment and hard labor over freedom in the hopes of strengthening protection of the sovereignty of a nation to which he did not belong. After fighting removal for years with his every resource, John Ross then requested to be its conductor. There is all of the majesty of Tsali's martyrdom for this people's liberty, regardless of the story's authenticity; and all of the degradation of the Georgia land lottery, in which state citizens vied to "win" their former neighbors' homes and lands. There is the power of Davy Crockett's refusal to support the Jackson administration's policy of removal, even though it meant his political career, and the horror of Elias Boudinot's mutilated body, defaced by his own people.

Some of the figures involved in the Trail of Tears story have particularly strong resonance in U.S. society today. Andrew Jackson, whose image appears on the $20 bill, remains on most historians' lists of great presidents, and recent efforts by scholars such as David and Jeanne Heidler and Andrew Burstein to temper the celebratory tone of previously published works on Jackson have created controversy.[2] In journalist Russ Braley's words, "Jackson was so admired that the song 'The Battle of New Orleans' can still be heard wherever radios play."[3] When Jackson's home, the Hermitage, was certified as an official site on the Historic Trail of Tears on March 15, 2006, the event marked what might become a starting point for a new, more three-dimensional and accurate assessment of Jackson's popular legacy.

The tale is all the more immediate and important because, in a real sense, the Trail of Tears story continues. While the United States expanded and exported its policy and self-image, the Cherokee Nation—or nations, as East and West were permanently sundered by the Trail of Tears—had little respite. In fact, the most shocking aspect of the removal story is that the dispossession of the Cherokee Nation did not end there. Despite U.S. treaty stipulations that the Indian Territory land belonged to the Cherokees in all perpetuity, this promise did not even last a lifetime. Immediately after the U.S. Civil War—during which many Cherokees fought for the Confederacy, in no small part because of that government's assurances of better protection for Cherokee rights—the United States limited the land rights of the native nations. In 1887, the Dawes Act, or Allotment Act, divided Cherokee land previously held in common into separate tracts for individual Cherokees. Not only did this dissolve all land for public, community use (such as governmental buildings), and uproot those who had made improvements to the property, but it also vastly decreased the total amount of land held by Cherokees, since tracts were of a standard size, and there was significant land left over after division. After assigning tracts, U.S. government officials opened the unassigned sections, not for Cherokees, but for white settlers. Thus Cherokee land was once again given away. According to the National Congress of American Indians, despite the Indian Reorganization Act's pledge to help restore the land base American Indians possessed in Indian Territory prior to 1887, less than 10 percent of the lands lost through allotment have returned to tribal control.[4]

In 1898, the Curtis Act abolished tribal courts. In 1907, statehood combined the Indian and Oklahoma territories by law, dissolving tribal governments. The Cherokees had fought Oklahoma statehood, just as they had fought every other encroachment on the land they had been forced to accept. At one point, some even attempted to gain statehood themselves as the state of Sequoyah, but the U.S. Congress denied the bid for statehood, and the constitution generated for the state of Sequoyah became the framework for the constitution of the state of Oklahoma.

Despite the fact that the Cherokee Nation of Oklahoma has since reorganized and institutionalized its national structure, as recently as 1997, the U.S. national government has continued its pattern of unauthorized, unlawful interference in Cherokee government—in that case, occupying the nation on behalf of a principal chief facing due process impeachment proceedings under Cherokee law. Although the Bureau of Indian Affairs later admitted wrongdoing, the agency did not retreat until grave damage was done to the Cherokee judicial process and law enforcement system. Meanwhile, investigations continue regarding alleged mismanagement of funds held in trust for native nations by the Bureau of Indian Affairs.[5] In the interim, under the 1976 Indian Self-Determination and Education Assistance Act and its recent amendments, American Indians such as the Cherokees must compete against each other for limited funds in a system that is at best unclear and at worst catastrophically mismanaged.[6]

In the face of such challenges, it is perhaps no surprise that the Cherokees have created a new literacy revolution, moving their preservation and study of the Cherokee language to the Internet. Downloadable Cherokee fonts, online tutorials, and teaching materials ensure that knowledge of the Cherokee language passes to new generations. For example, the Cherokee Nation Cultural Resource Center provides multiple language services to Cherokees and non-Cherokees alike, including community classes, teacher certification, and curriculum development, as well as Web-based courses.[7] Auburn University likewise sponsors the Echota Tsalagi Language Revitalization Project, which offers a multimedia educational experience complete with audio and video components to teach the Cherokee language.[8] What the Cherokee language means for Cherokee identity and sovereignty remains, as it did in the nineteenth century, a question with multiple answers and long-term implications.

While the language promotes pride in and appreciation of the rich Cherokee tradition, it also emphasizes the fact that the Cherokees are a people apart from the rest of the United States and the rest of Native America—made different not only by culture, but by the experience and memory of the Trail Where They Cried. The Cherokees also remain a people apart from each other; it is significant to note that the sundering of the Cherokees caused by the Trail of Tears has led to different dialects being spoken by Cherokees in the East and the West.

Of removal, Elias Boudinot once wrote that it was the least of all bad options, and perhaps the sole chance for Cherokee survival: "Removal, then, is the only remedy—the only practicable remedy. By it there may be finally a renovation—our people may rise from their very ashes to become prosperous and happy, and a credit to our race. Such has been and is now my opinion, and under such a settled opinion I have acted in all this affair. My language has been, 'fly for your lives'—it is now the same."[9] He did not say, however, what safe destination remained.

Notes

1. See the Primary Documents section.
2. Amy H. Sturgis, "Not the Same Old Hickory: The Contested Legacy of Andrew Jackson," *Reason*, May 2004, pp. 58–63.

3. Russ Braley, review of *Old Hickory's War: Andrew Jackson and the Quest for Empire*, by David Stephen Heidler, *Presidential Studies Quarterly* 26 (Summer 1996): 893–895, 893.

4. Matthew L. M. Fletcher, "The Insidious Colonialism of the Conqueror: The Federal Government in Modern Tribal Affairs," *Washington University Journal of Law and Policy*, 2005, available at http://ssrn.com/abstract=646981 (accessed May 10, 2006).

5. Amy H. Sturgis, "Tale of Tears," *Reason*, March 1999, pp. 46–52.

6. Elizabeth M. Glazer, "Appropriating Availability: Reconciling Purpose and Text under the Indian Self-Determination and Education Assistance Act," *University of Chicago Law Review* 71 (Fall 2004): 1637–1660. See also "Indian Self-Determination Act: Shortfalls in Indian Contract Support Costs Need to Be Addressed," June 1999, GAO/RCED-99-150 (Washington, DC: U.S. General Accounting Office, 1999).

7. http://www.cherokee.org/home.aspx?section=culture&culture=language (accessed May 10, 2006).

8. http://www.auburn.edu/outreach/dl/echota/index.php (accessed May 10, 2006).

9. Elias Boudinot, "Letters and Other Sundry Papers Relating to Cherokee Affairs: Being a Reply to Sundry Publications Authorized by John Ross by Elias Boudinot, Formerly Editor of the Cherokee Phoenix," in *Cherokee Editor: The Writings of Elias Boudinot*, ed. Theda Perdue (Athens: University of Georgia Press, 1996), pp. 159–225, 225.

Sequoyah with the Cherokee syllabary he created in 1821, which enabled Cherokee to become a written language. (Courtesy of Library of Congress)

Elias Boudinot, editor of *The Cherokee Phoenix* and one of the leaders of the Treaty Party. (OHS Glass Plate Collection, reproduced by permission of the Archives and Manuscripts Division of the Oklahoma Historical Society, 19615.43)

John Ross, principal chief of the Cherokee Nation during the Trail of Tears. (Courtesy of Library of Congress)

Andrew Jackson, the seventh president of the United States and the architect of Indian removal. (Courtesy of Library of Congress)

Major Ridge, an elder statesman of the Cherokee Nation and a key member of the Treaty Party. (Courtesy of Library of Congress)

John Ridge, son of Major Ridge and member of the Treaty Party, which was responsible for the Treaty of New Echota. (Courtesy of Library of Congress)

Martin Van Buren, the eighth president of the United States, during whose
administration the Trail of Tears took place. (Courtesy of Library of Congress)

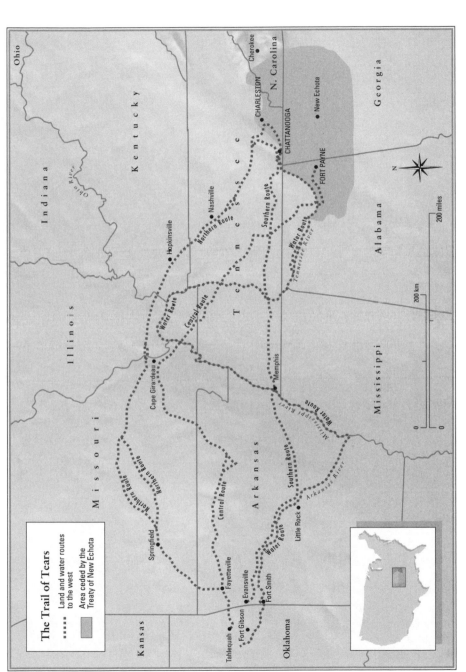

The various routes that made up the Trail of Tears during the removal of the Cherokee Nation.

BIOGRAPHIES

Elias Boudinot (c. 1804–June 22, 1839)

Editor of *The Cherokee Phoenix* and Leader of the Treaty Party

Elias Boudinot is perhaps best known for negotiating and signing the Treaty of New Echota in 1835, which exchanged the lands of the Cherokee Nation for other lands west of the Mississippi. The U.S. government used the agreement's two-year provision for voluntary relocation as a cue to begin forced removal in 1838. Boudinot paid with his life for signing the compact many blamed as a primary cause of the Trail of Tears. Boudinot was also an editor, a writer, a translator, and an activist for the causes of Christianity and temperance.

Boudinot was born Buck Watie, or Galagina, at Oothcaloga in the Cherokee Nation in or around the year 1804. His life was inextricably tied with that of his uncle, The Ridge (later Major Ridge) and cousin, John Ridge, who, like his own family, lived not in the traditional Cherokee town of Hiwassee, but rather on a large, individual farm, much like many U.S. citizens in the South. Buck Watie attended a Moravian mission school beginning in 1811, and in 1818, he received an invitation from the interdenominational association known as the American Board of Commissioners for Foreign Missions to study at the Foreign Mission School in Cornwall, Connecticut, as did his cousin John. En route to the New England school, Watie met Elias Boudinot, leader of the American Bible Society and former member of the Continental Congress. The statesman and religious figure made a tremendous impression on Watie, and when he reached the Foreign Mission School, he enrolled under the name Elias Boudinot.

At the Foreign Mission School, Boudinot converted to Christianity and considered attending seminary. The school used him as a student spokesman, an impressive example of the benefits of educating American Indians. When he married Harriet Ruggles Gold, the white daughter of a Cornwall physician, in 1826, however, he was no longer a celebrated favorite. The outraged school agents closed the institution lest any other interracial unions be encouraged. The marriage of Boudinot's cousin, John Ridge, to another white woman inspired similar horror among many white New Englanders. Such bitter experiences led Boudinot to distrust the United States and its mainstream population, even as he continued to embrace the "civilization" agenda.

Boudinot returned to the Cherokee Nation, where he served as clerk for the Cherokee Nation during the creation of the 1827 constitution. He raised funds for a Cherokee printing press by touring the United States and lecturing about the state and promise of Cherokee society. The collected funds made possible *The Cherokee Phoenix*, the first Cherokee newspaper, a bilingual publication printed in both Cherokee and English. Boudinot became its editor. He continued to be involved with temperance and Christian organizations and linguistic pursuits, and translated the religious tract *Poor Sarah, or The Indian Woman* into Cherokee. With his friend, white missionary Samuel Worcester, Boudinot also translated the New Testament and various traditional hymns.

Boudinot became a staunch supporter of Cherokee rights. He published many editorials in *The Cherokee Phoenix* about the escalating tensions with the state of Georgia, which culminated in the Supreme Court case *Worcester v. Georgia*. When the Georgia state government and the U.S. president both chose to ignore the court's decision, which favored the Cherokee Nation, Boudinot's perspective on removal began to change. He eventually believed the choice that faced Cherokees was not between living on Cherokee lands or leaving, but rather leaving or facing extermination. Boudinot, along with Major and John Ridge, proposed trying to negotiate for favorable removal terms. Most Cherokees opposed any thought of removal, however. The Cherokee government, wishing the Cherokees to maintain a united front in the face of the crisis, prohibited debate in the Cherokee paper about removal. In response, Boudinot resigned as editor. Along with like-minded Cherokees such as the Ridges, and his brother, Stand Watie, Boudinot arranged to meet with representatives of the United States. Despite the fact that he lacked any authority to do so, and such action was punishable by death under Cherokee law, Boudinot signed the Treaty of New Echota in 1835. The U.S. Senate ratified the agreement by one vote. U.S. forces used this treaty to justify the forced removal known as the Trail of Tears.

In 1837, Boudinot voluntarily moved his household to Park Hill, in present-day Oklahoma. He was widely criticized and ostracized for his actions. Two years later, he was attacked at his home and mortally wounded by a group of unidentified Cherokee assailants. His uncle and cousin, who also had signed the Treaty of New Echota, likewise were killed on the same day. His brother, Stand Watie, survived an attack on his life on the same day, and blamed John Ross and his supporters for the deaths. He engaged in a long-running feud with the Ross camp, and is best known as the only Native American Confederate soldier to earn the rank of General, and the last Confederate General to surrender after the U.S. Civil War.

Andrew Jackson (March 15, 1767–June 8, 1845)

Seventh President of the United States

Andrew Jackson was a founder of the Democratic Party and the inspiration for the Jacksonian revolution, a series of reform movements that followed from his example and rhetoric as an egalitarian and common man. Jackson, a lawyer and planter in Tennessee, was known for his passionate temper and rage, which led him to challenge men to duels and sometimes even kill them. He earned the nickname "Old Hickory" by his toughness as a soldier. His military career included successful campaigns against the Red Stick Creeks and Seminoles, as well as a stunning victory during the War of 1812 in the Battle of New Orleans, which made him a national hero. Jackson cultivated his military reputation as an "Indian fighter." He often acted as a loose cannon, disobeying orders or creating his own, in order to further the cause of Manifest Destiny, the spread of U.S. control over the North American continent. One of the main obstacles to settlement and expansion, in Jackson's eyes, was the native peoples, including the Cherokee Nation.

In the election of 1828, Jackson rode his status as a war hero and frontiersman for the common man all the way to the White House. During his two terms as president, Jackson was best known for championing the spoils system of political patronage, ending the National Bank, and engaging with South Carolina in the Nullification Crisis. Jackson's other most visible act was setting the stage for the Trail of Tears and Indian removal. Jackson's approach to the "Indian question" effectively ended the era of the Indian "civilization" program, which had marked U.S. policy toward native nations since

George Washington's administration. When the U.S. Supreme Court decided in favor of the Cherokee Nation in *Worcester v. Georgia*, Jackson ignored the judiciary and refused to interfere with Georgia's oppression of the Cherokee Nation. He supported the Indian Removal Act of 1830, and pushed for other native nations to move to the West. When the Cherokee Nation would not negotiate removal treaties, Jackson recognized the illegitimate Treaty of New Echota that had been made by the minority Ridge-Boudinot Party without authority. Although the Trail of Tears itself did not occur until the administration of Martin Van Buren, Jackson's former vice president and hand-picked successor, Jackson was responsible for providing the key ingredients necessary for removal to take place.

One of the greatest contradictions in Jackson's story is the tension between his self-reliance and distrust of authority and privilege, and his actions that accumulated power not in the hands of the common people, but in the institution of the national government, and especially the executive branch. He made the political personal, and he backed the idea of Manifest Destiny with laws and guns. In the end, reformers involved in the rising swell of "Jacksonian" movements such as feminism, abolitionism, and Transcendentalism actively protested Jackson's policy of removal, to no avail.

John Marshall (September 24, 1755–July 6, 1835)

Chief Justice of the U.S. Supreme Court

The oldest of fifteen children born to planter John Marshall and his wife Mary in Germantown, Virginia, John Marshall made an impact on U.S. history as a statesman, attorney, legislator, and soldier. He served as a Virginia delegate, U.S. representative, special emissary to France, and secretary of state. He is best remembered as the fourth chief justice of the U.S. Supreme Court, a position he held for over thirty years. In that role he shaped U.S. constitutional law and established the power of judicial review.

Marshall penned the majority opinion in two cases that related directly to the question of Cherokee removal. The first was the 1831 decision for *Cherokee Nation v. Georgia*. The Cherokee Nation brought this case against the state of Georgia in response to several policies the state had enacted. For example, the state government redrew the boundaries of Georgia counties so they would include previously identified Cherokee land. The state also extended its laws over the Cherokees, in effect dissolving the Cherokee Nation's sovereignty as a separate political body. Finally, Georgia lawmakers devised a lottery system to redistribute Cherokee land to Georgia citizens. In their case before the court, the Cherokees claimed that the Georgia state laws violated international treaties that the United States had made with the Cherokees. Marshall responded that the treaties with the Cherokee Nation were not technically international treaties, because native nations were "domestic dependent nations." His sympathy for the Cherokees' position was clear, however, and his receptiveness encouraged them to bring another case before the court.

The second case was 1832's *Worcester v. Georgia*. In this case, white missionary Samuel Worcester sued the state of Georgia for trying to extend its laws over the Cherokee Nation. Georgia had passed an act that required all whites who lived within the Cherokee Nation to apply for a state permit and swear an oath of allegiance to Georgia. Worcester was one of several ministers from the American Board of Commissioners for Foreign Missions who refused to follow the Georgia act and subsequently were arrested, tried in a Georgia court, convicted, and sentenced to four years of hard labor. This time the Supreme Court felt it had the jurisdiction necessary to support the Cherokees. In the opinion he drafted for the case, Marshall argued that relations with native nations were the realm of the national government, and a state had no right to interfere with a group the United States had already recognized and agreed to protect. This decision brought temporary hope and lasting credibility to the Cherokee fight against removal, but, in the end, was not enough to prevent the Trail of Tears.

Major Ridge, also known as The Ridge (c. 1771– June 22, 1839)

Leader of the Treaty Party

Major Ridge, best known for his role in the Treaty of New Echota, was originally called the Pathkiller. He was born one of six children at Hiwassee, in what is now Polk County, Tennessee. His mother was half Cherokee, and his father was a Scottish frontiersman. As a man he was known first as The Ridge, and later as Major Ridge, after earning the rank of major while fighting with U.S. forces led by Andrew Jackson against the Red Stick Creeks. The Ridge's life spanned a crucial period in Cherokee acculturation; as a young man he was trained as a hunter and warrior, but he eventually became a wealthy plantation farmer not unlike his U.S. neighbors in the South. He and his family eventually settled in the Oothcaloga Valley in Georgia.

The Ridge held many positions of leadership among his fellow Cherokees. While serving as ambassador to the Creek Confederation, he was adopted as a chief and offered a seat on the Creek council. He helped to gather Cherokee troops to fight with the United States against Great Britain and later the Red Stick Creeks. He represented the Cherokee Nation on multiple trips to Washington, D.C., and helped ally Creeks to negotiate a treaty with the United States. In 1827 he temporarily served as the head of the Cherokee Nation until the 1828 election of John Ross, under whom he served as first councilor.

After the Indian Removal Act of 1830, Major Ridge, like his son John Ridge and nephew Elias Boudinot—both of whom had studied at the Foreign Mission School in Cornwall, Connecticut, and returned to the Cherokee Nation to join the next generation of its leaders—began to fear that removal was inevitable, or at least necessary for Cherokee survival. Major Ridge observed firsthand how the state of Georgia began to transfer Cherokee property to Georgia citizens through a lottery system while debate about the Cherokee situation continued for months and then years in Washington, D.C. At length Major Ridge, his son, his nephew, and others decided that desperate measures were necessary to make sure the Cherokees salvaged whatever possible from a situation that continually worsened. They met with U.S. representatives and, without authority, agreed to the Treaty of New Echota, which ceded Cherokee lands in the East for lands in the West. He knew the act carried with it a death sentence; in fact, the situation held particular dramatic irony for Major Ridge for two reasons. First, he had been among the group of Cherokees who had carried out Chief Doublehead's execution years earlier for the same trespass. Second, John Ridge had been the one to write the death sentence into law under the new Cherokee Constitution.

An ailing Major Ridge relocated to Indian Territory in 1837, where he declined to take further part in Cherokee politics. One year later, the Trail of Tears began. Many blamed Major Ridge and his Treaty Party for the devastation and death caused by removal. On June 22, 1839, Major Ridge was attacked by unknown Cherokee assailants and killed; his son John Ridge and nephew Elias Boudinot met the same fate.

John Ross (October 3, 1790–August 1, 1866)

Principal Chief of the Cherokee Nation

Repeatedly elected to the Cherokee Nation's highest office, John Ross was the principal chief of the Cherokee Nation during its greatest crisis, the Trail of Tears. He was born in Turkey Town in the Cherokee Nation, near what is today Center, Alabama. His father and grandfathers were Scottish traders who married Cherokee wives; in Ross's early days, he seemed to follow in their tradition. He entered the merchandising business, operating a ferry and warehouse at Ross's Landing (contemporary Chattanooga, Tennessee), before becoming a plantation farmer and one of the richest men in the Cherokee Nation.

Even though he was a mixed-blood with little connection to the Cherokee language, Ross had the trust of many traditional fullblood Cherokees as well as those like himself who were more inclined toward acculturation with white society. He began his involvement in Cherokee politics as a clerk and a tribal delegate to Washington, D.C., in 1816. In three years he was the leader of the Cherokee legislature. In 1827, Ross was elected president of the Cherokee Constitutional Convention, in which he helped to frame the final document that would be adopted by the nation. He became the first principal chief elected under the new constitution, and he was continually reelected to that position—first in the original Cherokee Nation east of the Mississippi River and, after the Trail of Tears, in Indian Territory—until his death in 1866. He was married twice. His first marriage, in 1813, was to a Cherokee woman named Quatie (or Elizabeth Brown Henley), with whom he had six children; she died on the Trail of Tears in 1839. He married a second time in 1844, this time to a white Quaker woman from Delaware named Mary Brian Stapler, who was thirty-five years his junior. They had two children before she died in 1865.

As principal chief, Ross worked continuously against removal, writing letters, making speeches, delivering petitions, and working in Washington, D.C., trying to make the Cherokee position heard. His efforts bore some fruit, and positive events did occur, such as the pro-Cherokee 1832 *Worcester v. Georgia* decision from the U.S. Supreme Court and the rise of protests against removal from reform groups and intellectual leaders across the country. But the Removal Act of 1830, and the continued efforts of Georgia, sanctioned by President Andrew Jackson, eventually led a minority of Cherokees to seek a treaty. The 1835 Treaty of New Echota was neither legally legitimate nor representative of the Cherokee majority will, but it was a necessary ingredient for the Trail of Tears, and the U.S. national government ratified and accepted it. Ross challenged the treaty under both the Jackson and Van Buren administrations to no avail.

After the Trail of Tears began, and resistance was no longer viable, Ross convinced General Winfield Scott to allow the Cherokee National Council to oversee the removal operations, and although the consequences of the marches were devastating, the condition of the Cherokee-led contingents proved more humane than those conducted by the U.S. military. After reaching Indian Territory, Ross was instrumental in the ratification and adoption of a new Cherokee Constitution in 1839, and a new U.S. treaty in 1846. For his enduring devotion to his people and their cause, Ross remained a unifying figure and beloved leader. He died while still in office in 1866.

Winfield Scott (June 13, 1786–May 29, 1866)

U.S. Army General

Historians often consider Winfield Scott the greatest military commander of his era; he served actively as a general longer than any other person in U.S. history. Known as "Old Fuss and Feathers" for his emphasis on military discipline and appearance, and "Grand Old Man of the Army" for his great longevity and reputation, Scott was the first U.S. soldier after George Washington to earn the rank of lieutenant general. He was also a military governor, diplomat, presidential candidate, and revered public figure.

Born near Petersburg, Virginia, on his family's farm, Scott practiced law and belonged to the Virginia militia before joining the U.S. Army. He went on to serve in the War of 1812, the Mexican-American War, and the U.S. Civil War, in which he introduced the Anaconda Plan that was responsible for defeating the Confederate Army. Scott also played a role in several key Native American conflicts, including the Black Hawk War and Second Seminole War.

In 1838, President Martin Van Buren ordered Scott to take control of the Cherokee removal campaign. Scott was dismayed when he learned the attitude of some of the militia troops who formed the 7,000-man removal force. He especially feared violence from some of the Georgia soldiers and tried to oversee their handling of the Cherokees in particular. He addressed the Cherokees and conveyed his desire for a peaceful relocation; he also gave instructions to his men to treat their prisoners humanely.

He organized the removal effort into three military regions with different holding camps, launch points, and routes of travel. Despite his best intentions, however, the roundup and first wave of marches were anything but smooth and humane. Thousands died in the containment camps because of the inadequate facilities, disease, and drought conditions. More died en route to Indian Country. After these first calamities, Scott delayed the removal process, even though this action earned vocal protest from pro-removal forces, including former president Andrew Jackson. When Principal Chief John Ross petitioned for Cherokee control of the removal process, Scott readily agreed. Scott also played a role in the Tsali story, as the instigator of the agreement by which Tsali and his sons were executed for the deaths of U.S. soldiers, and in return all other fugitive Cherokees hiding from removal in the Smoky Mountains were left at liberty. Scott died in the town of West Point, New York, a popular U.S. hero.

Sequoyah (c. 1770–1843)

Inventor of the Cherokee Syllabary

Sequoyah is perhaps one of the most celebrated Native American figures in the world. He never knew his white father, but his Cherokee mother traced her descent from several notable chiefs. A farmer, soldier (in the war against the Red Stick Creeks), blacksmith, and silversmith, Sequoyah was the inventor of the Cherokee syllabary in 1821, which almost overnight created a literacy revolution in the Cherokee Nation and forever transformed Cherokee society.

He was alternately thought stupid, insane, and a practitioner of witchcraft by his neighbors, and his wife even burned the first drafts of his work to dissuade him from his eccentric experiments. But Sequoyah was inspired by the "talking leaves" of the U.S. culture and wanted to create a similar tool for Cherokees. With help from his daughter Ahyokeh, Sequoyah eventually produced a syllabary of eighty-five characters. Although the symbols were significantly larger in number than the letters of the English alphabet, the syllabary system proved an extremely efficient means of transforming the spoken language into a written form. It required only days to learn and master. Sequoyah unveiled his creation in 1821. Soon it was the focus of national attention among Cherokees, and only four years later, a majority of Cherokees were able to read and write in the new "Sequoyan" system.

The literacy revolution at the time was a potent political and cultural event. It allowed for the creation of a bilingual Cherokee press, *The Cherokee Phoenix*, and the dissemination of everything from laws to Christian religious tracts. The invention showcased the "civilized" nature of the Cherokees to those outside the Cherokee Nation, while also allowing for a clear cultural separation between the Cherokees and the United States. The language and the revolution it created also drew the lines from which full-scale factions arose during the last days of the removal controversy, between those who favored separatism and those who favored assimilationism with regard to the United States.

Sequoyah and his family voluntarily emigrated to what was known as Arkansas Territory in 1822, and thus were absent from much of the public reaction, both Cherokee and U.S., to his creation, although he later accepted a medal from the Legislative Council of the Cherokee Nation in honor of his achievement. Because of his move, he was not forced to endure the Trail of Tears personally. He was an established Old Settler by the time removal brought thousands of displaced Cherokees to Indian Territory. In 1838, he became an advocate for political unity between the newly arrived survivors of the Trail of Tears and the established Old Settlers. The dream of bringing together Cherokees in unity eventually led him to join a group who set out in 1843 to find another branch of Cherokees who were believed to be in northern Mexico. The party became lost, and then divided while seeking for help, and Sequoyah was never seen again. His syllabary continues to play an important role in Cherokee culture and identity today, and to symbolize Native American intellectual achievement. When several combined native nations attempted to secure statehood for Indian Territory in the first decade of the twentieth century, the would-be state was named Sequoyah. The U.S. Congress denied the petition for statehood, but the constitution drafted for Sequoyah eventually became the basis for the Oklahoma state constitution.

Tsali (unknown–November 1838)

Cherokee Martyr

Much of Tsali's story remains a mystery. In 1838, was he a sixty-year-old grandfather, or a young bachelor? Was he defending his wife against abuse from U.S. soldiers, or simply trying to escape? In fact, the details of Tsali's story may be less relevant than the potency of his legend, which continues to be the source of contemporary literature and drama, and a symbol of Cherokee endurance and sacrifice during the Trail of Tears.

The traditional account of the story of Tsali, or Charley, is that he and his family were Cherokees who were taken by force from their homes in North Carolina by U.S. troops in 1838 so that they, with the rest of the Cherokee Nation, could be moved to Indian Territory. When the soldiers were abusive to Tsali's wife, Tsali and his sons retaliated in her defense, killing one or more of the soldiers. Tsali and his family, as well as the other Cherokees taken in their group, fled into the Smoky Mountains. There they were joined by additional refugees from removal.

According to the tale, General Winfield Scott, who supervised the removal process on behalf of the United States, offered a deal: if the Cherokees would surrender Tsali and his party, no other Cherokees currently in hiding would be pursued any further. Tsali and his oldest sons therefore came forward of their own free will, sacrificing their lives for the freedom of the rest of the fugitive Cherokees.

Tsali's story contains disturbing elements. Was Tsali guilty, if acting in self-defense for himself or his wife? Did other Cherokees betray his whereabouts in order to save themselves? It seems clear from official reports that U.S. troops forced other Cherokees to act as executioners for Tsali and his sons. But the Tsali story also wrests dignity and control from a degrading and desperate episode in Cherokee history. The idea of the martyr sacrificing himself and his family for his people speaks to the Cherokee values of unity, loyalty, and courage, and allows for a moment of victory, albeit a bittersweet one, in the midst of tragedy. Tsali's story remains central to the Eastern band of Cherokees, who memorialize it in the drama *Unto These Hills.*

Martin Van Buren (December 5, 1782–July 24, 1862)

Eighth President of the United States

Born in Kinderhook, New York, Martin Van Buren was the descendent of Dutch immigrants; in fact, his first language was Dutch, which made him the only U.S. president whose first language was not English. He became an attorney and practiced law for twenty-five years in his native New York, where state politics were contentious following the dissolution of the first party system. Van Buren, along with Andrew Jackson, helped frame the second party system through the Democratic-Republican, later Democratic, party.

Van Buren moved steadily up from state to national politics, serving as a state senator, U.S. senator, governor of New York, and secretary of state before replacing John C. Calhoun as Andrew Jackson's vice president. After Jackson completed his second term, Van Buren was elected to the nation's highest office. Committed to the "common man" rhetoric of the Jacksonian revolution, Van Buren vowed to follow in Jackson's footsteps and continue his policies. He only changed one member of Jackson's cabinet. But Jackson's legacies were not all positive, and Van Buren soon found himself in a desperate situation, in the midst of the second worst depression the United States has ever endured.

The Panic of 1837 followed shortly after Van Buren took office. The panic itself originated in New York City, where the banks ceased payment in gold and silver. What followed was five years of economic depression. Van Buren, renamed "Van Ruin" by his opponents, fought members of his own party as well as the Whigs to implement an "Independent Treasury" system to respond to the crisis. Although he received his party's nomination for the election of 1840, Van Buren lost the presidency to William Henry Harrison. For a time he seemed poised to gain the nomination for the 1844 presidential race, but he failed to get two-thirds of the convention votes. The nomination went to the dark horse candidate James K. Polk instead. Van Buren was nominated by the "Barnburner" and "Free Soiler" factions of the party in 1848, but he received no electoral votes.

Although Andrew Jackson was primarily responsible for setting the stage for Cherokee removal, the Trail of Tears took place during Van Buren's administration. On the one hand, he received petitions and protests from Cherokee and U.S. sources pleading with him to delay or stop the removal process; on the other hand, state leaders such as Georgia Governor George Gilmer pressed him for a more vigorous commitment to removal. In the end, Van Buren answered with relative inaction, allowing events to unfold as Jackson had imagined. Perhaps because he was not an "Indian fighter" president, or the one who set the stage for removal, Van Buren's role, even if it was a mostly passive one, is often overlooked. Andrew Jackson continues to be the president most closely linked with the Trail of Tears.

Samuel Worcester (January 19, 1798–April 20, 1859)

Plaintiff in *Worcester v. Georgia*

Minister, missionary, translator, and activist, Samuel Worcester played a key role in the life of the Cherokee Nation. Born to a family composed of six generations of preachers, Worcester was studying in New England to become the seventh when he met Cherokee student Elias Boudinot. The two became lifelong friends and colleagues. When Worcester became a member of the American Board of Commissioners for Foreign Missions, he requested that he be assigned to serve in the Cherokee Nation. He was sent to a needy community Boudinot had suggested near present-day Brainerd, Tennessee, where he fulfilled the role of preacher, teacher, and translator, as well as sometimes doctor, carpenter, and blacksmith. His affinity for languages allowed him to become part of the Cherokee community.

After the introduction of Sequoyah's syllabary, Worcester played a critical role in helping Elias Boudinot raise funds for a printing press and all of the equipment and supplies necessary for a printing office—including casting of the Cherokee syllabary so it could be typeset. Thus *The Cherokee Phoenix*, the bilingual newspaper, was born. Worcester wrote about Cherokee linguistics and collaborated with Boudinot on various translations of English religious texts into Cherokee editions.

Worcester was one of several missionaries who protested when the state of Georgia violated Cherokee national sovereignty by passing a law that required all non-Cherokees to get a license from Georgia in order to work within the Cherokee Nation. He was arrested by the Georgia militia, tried and convicted, and sentenced to four years of hard labor. His case was heard by the U.S. Supreme Court, and in the 1832 *Worcester v. Georgia* decision, Chief Justice Marshall and his colleagues agreed that the Cherokee Nation was independent, and no state could dissolve or infringe upon it. It was a great victory for the Cherokee Nation, but because both the Georgia state government and the president of the United States ignored the decision, it was a hollow one.

Eventually freed from his imprisonment, Worcester moved to Indian Territory in 1835. He believed that removal was inevitable, and he wanted to prepare for the influx of Cherokees who would make their way West. Throughout the turbulent times of the Cherokee political factionalism, Worcester maintained his close friendship with Boudinot, who became a controversial figure because of his involvement with the Treaty of New Echota. The two continued to work together on Cherokee publications, and after Elias Boudinot also moved West, he planned to build a house for his family near Worcester so that the two could continue their collaborations. Boudinot was staying with Worcester during the new house's construction on June 22, 1839, when assailants attacked and killed him for his role in the Trail of Tears. A messenger from Worcester's home warned Boudinot's brother Stand Watie in time to spare him a similar fate. Worcester's dedication to the Cherokee people continued until his death in 1866.

PRIMARY DOCUMENTS

Document 1: Petition of Cherokee Women, June 30, 1818

Most of the Cherokee debate about removal involved men. Cherokee society before European colonization originally had been matriarchal in structure, but the Cherokees had changed their governmental and social systems as part of their adaptation to Western practices and values. Exposure to Christianity, as well as to colonial and then U.S. political practices, had inspired this change. Nevertheless, women continued to play an important role in Cherokee life. One of the most celebrated women of the late eighteenth and early nineteenth century was Nancy Ward, who had earned the title of Cherokee Beloved Woman when she rallied Cherokee troops in battle in 1755. She went on to help General George Washington's troops during the Revolutionary War and address the Hopewell Treaty conference. Ward's own life reflected the complexities of Cherokee acculturation; on the one hand, she was outspoken in her defense of her people and their rights, but on the other hand, she married a white man, owned African slaves, and dressed in U.S. fashion. In the 1818 "Petition of Cherokee Women," the aging Ward and other Cherokee women expressed their anxieties about the potential of removal. The women particularly emphasized the points of similarity—common faith, intermarriage—with their audience, while also underscoring their helplessness. (Source: Andrew Jackson Presidential Papers microfilm, Washington, DC, 1961, series 1, reel 22. Also cited in *The Cherokee Removal: A Brief History with Documents*, ed. Theda Perdue and Michael Green [New York: Bedford/St. Martin's, 1995], p. 125.)

Beloved Children,

We have called a meeting among ourselves to consult on the different points now before the council, relating to our national affairs. We have heard with painful feelings that the bounds of the land we now possess are to be drawn into very narrow limits. The land was given to us by the Great Spirit above as our common right, to raise our children upon, & to make support for our rising generations. We therefore humbly petition our beloved children, the head men & warriors, to hold out to the last in support of our common rights, as the Cherokee nation have been the first settlers of this land; we therefore claim the right of the soil.

We well remember that our country was formerly very extensive, but by repeated sales it has become circumscribed to the very narrow limits we have at present. Our Father the President advised us to become farmers, to manufacture our own clothes, & to have our children instructed. To this advice we have attended in every thing as far as we were able. Now the thought of being compelled to remove the other side of the Mississippi is dreadful to us, because it appears to us that we, by this removal, shall be brought to a savage state again, for we have, by the endeavor of our Father the President, become too much enlightened to throw aside the privileges of a civilized life.

We therefore unanimously join in our meeting to hold our country in common as hitherto.

Some of our children have become Christians. We have missionary schools among us. We have hard the gospel in our nation. We have become civilized & enlightened, & are in hopes that in a few years our nation will be prepared for instruction in other branches of sciences & arts, which are both useful & necessary in civilized society.

There are some white men among us who have been raised in this country from their youth, are connected with us by marriage, & have considerable families, who are very active in encouraging the emigration of our nation. These ought to be our truest friends but prove our worst enemies. They seem to be only concerned how to increase their riches, but do not care what becomes of our Nation, nor even of their own wives and children.

Document 2: The Indian Removal Act, May 28, 1830

The Indian Removal Act was a direct result of President Andrew Jackson's first State of the Union address in December 1829, which called for aggressive Indian removal policy for native nations in the East. The Committees on Indian Affairs in the U.S. Senate and House of Representatives—both of which were led by Tennessee Congressmen—generated similar bills in late February 1830. The Senate version prevailed. Debate about the Indian Removal Act divided, with few exceptions, along sectional lines. Those who opposed the act included mostly anti-Jackson Northerners such as Senators Peleg Sprague from Maine, Ascher Robbins from Rhode Island, and Theodore Frelinghuysen, who delivered a six-hour speech against the proposition. One notable Southerner who also disagreed with the measure was Representative Davy Crockett of Tennessee, whose opposition ultimately cost him his political career. Vocal proponents of the bill included senators such as John Forsyth of Georgia, Robert Adams of Mississippi, and committee chairman Hugh Lawson White of Tennessee. Because removal was an idea particularly important to Jackson, the debate became as much a referendum on his presidency as a conflict about Native America, and the debate was all the more passionate and bitter because of it. The vote was close in the House (102 to 97), but clear in the Senate (28 to 19). Signed into law on May 28, 1830, the Indian Removal Act set in motion the events directly leading to the Trail of Tears. (Source: Primary Documents in American History, Library of Congress Collection Guides and Bibliographies, available at http://www.loc.gov/rr/program/bib/ourdocs/Indian.html [accessed January 21, 2006].)

An Act to provide for an exchange of lands with the Indians residing in any of the states or territories, and for their removal west of the river Mississippi.

Be it enacted by the Senate and House of Representatives of the United States of America, in Congress assembled, That it shall and may be lawful for the President of the United States to cause so much of any territory belonging to the United States, west of the river Mississippi, not included in any state or organized territory, and to which the Indian title has been extinguished, as he may judge necessary, to be divided into a suitable number of districts, for the reception of such tribes or nations of Indians as may choose to exchange the lands where they now reside, and remove there; and to cause each of said districts to be so described by natural or artificial marks, as to be easily distinguished from every other.

Sec. 2 *And be it further enacted,* That it shall and may be lawful for the President to exchange any or all of such districts, so to be laid off and described, with any tribe or nation of Indians now residing within the limits of any of the states or territories, and with which the United States have existing treaties, for the whole or any part or portion of the territory claimed and occupied by such tribe or nation, within the bounds of any one or more of the states or territories, where the land claimed and occupied by the Indians, is owned by the United States, or the United States are bound to the state within which it lies to extinguish the Indian claim thereto.

Sec. 3 *And be it further enacted*, That in the making of any such exchange or exchanges, it shall and may be lawful for the President solemnly to assure the tribe or nation with which the exchange is made, that the United States will forever secure and guarantee to them, and their heirs or successors, the country so exchanged with them; and if they prefer it, that the United States will cause a patent or grant to be made and executed to them for the same: *Provided always*, That such lands shall revert to the United States, if the Indians become extinct, or abandon the same.

Sec. 4 *And be it further enacted*, That if, upon any of the lands now occupied by the Indians, and to be exchanged for, there should be such improvements as add value to the land claimed by any individual or individuals of such tribes or nations, it shall and may be lawful for the President to cause such value to be ascertained by appraisement or otherwise, and to cause such ascertained value to be paid to the person or persons rightfully claiming such improvements. And upon the payment of such valuation, the improvements so valued and paid for, shall pass to the United States, and possession shall not afterwards be permitted to any of the same tribe.

Sec. 5 *And be it further enacted*, That upon the making of any such exchange as is contemplated by this act, it shall and may be lawful for the President to cause such aid and assistance to be furnished to the emigrants as may be necessary and proper to enable them to remove to, and settle in, the country for which they may have exchanged; and also, to give them such aid and assistance as may be necessary for their support and subsistence for the first year after their removal.

Sec. 6 *And be it further enacted*, That it shall and may be lawful for the President to cause such tribe or nation to be protected, at their new residence, against all interruption or disturbance from any other tribe or nation of Indians, or from any other person or persons whatever.

Sec. 7 *And be it further enacted*, That it shall and may be lawful for the President to have the same superintendence and care over any tribe or nation in the country to which they may remove, as contemplated by this act, that he is now authorized to have over them at their present places of residence: *Provided*, That nothing in this act contained shall be construed as authorizing or directing the violation of any existing treaty between the United States and any of the Indian tribes.

Sec. 8 *And be it further enacted*, That for the purpose of giving effect to the provisions of this act, the sum of five hundred thousand dollars is hereby appropriated, to be paid out of any money in the treasury, not otherwise appropriated.

Document 3: Andrew Jackson's Second Annual Message to Congress, December 6, 1830

In his second State of the Union address, President Andrew Jackson was self-congratulatory about one of the products of his first State of the Union address: the 1830 Indian Removal Act. By explaining the virtues of removal, Jackson in his second annual address thanked the congressmen who put his ideas in action; by predicting the act's success and encouraging others to support its supposedly humanitarian mission, Jackson tried to appeal to his opponents. One of the key features of this speech is the signature paternalism Jackson showed toward the native nations. His rhetoric suggested that the American Indians did not know what was good for them, and it was the responsibility of the United States to act for their own good, by force if necessary. He also attempted to portray the Indian Removal Act as the next natural step in U.S. Indian policy. Cherokee leaders such as John Ross and Elias Boudinot disagreed, and in their writings were clear that removal was a rever-sal of the policies of previous administrations, such as those of George Washington and Thomas Jefferson. (Source: Andrew Jackson Speeches, Miller Center of Public Affairs, Scripps Library and Multimedia Archive, available at http://millercenter.virginia.edu/scripps/diglibrary/prezspeeches/jackson/aj_1830_1206.html [accessed December 15, 2005].)

It gives me pleasure to announce to Congress that the benevo-lent policy of the Government, steadily pursued for nearly 30 years, in relation to the removal of the Indians beyond the white settlements is approaching to a happy consummation. Two im-portant tribes have accepted the provision made for their re-moval at the last session of Congress, and it is believed that their example will induce the remaining tribes also to seek the same obvious advantages.

The consequences of a speedy removal will be important to the United States, to individual States, and to the Indians themselves. The pecuniary advantages which it promises to the Government are the least of its recommendations. It puts an end to all possible danger of collision between the authorities of the General and State Governments on account of the Indians. It will place a dense and civilized population in large tracts of country now occupied by a few savage hunters. By opening the whole territory between Tennessee on the north and Louisiana on the south to the settlement of the whites it will incalculably strengthen the SW frontier and render the adjacent States strong enough to repel future invasions without remote aid. It will relieve the whole State of Mississippi and the western part of Alabama of Indian occupancy, and enable those States to advance rapidly in population, wealth, and power. It will separate the Indians from immediate contact with settlements of whites; free them from the power of the States; enable them to pursue happiness in their own way and under their own rude institutions; will retard the progress of decay, which is lessening their numbers, and perhaps cause them gradually, under the protection of the Government and through the influence of good counsels, to cast off their savage habits and become an interesting, civilized, and Christian community. These consequences, some of them so certain and the rest so probable, make the complete execution of the plan sanctioned by Congress at their last session an object of much solicitude.

Toward the aborigines of the country no one can indulge a more friendly feeling than myself, or would go further in attempting to reclaim them from their wandering habits and make them a happy, prosperous people. I have endeavored to impress upon them my own solemn convictions of the duties and powers of the General Government in relation to the State authorities. For the justice of the laws passed by the States within the scope of their reserved powers they are not responsible to this Government. As individuals we may entertain and express our opinions of their acts, but as a Government we have as little right to control them as we have to prescribe laws for other nations.

With a full understanding of the subject, the Choctaw and the Chickasaw tribes have with great unanimity determined to avail themselves of the liberal offers presented by the act of Congress, and have agreed to remove beyond the Mississippi River. Treaties have been made with them, which in due season will be submitted for consideration. In negotiating these treaties they were made to understand their true condition, and they have preferred maintaining their independence in the Western forests to submitting to the laws of the States in which they now reside. These treaties, being probably the last which will ever be made with them, are characterized by great liberality on the part of the Government. They give the Indians a liberal sum in consideration of their removal, and comfortable subsistence on their arrival at their new homes. If it be their real interest to maintain a separate existence, they will there be at liberty to do so without the inconveniences and vexations to which they would unavoidably have been subject in Alabama and Mississippi.

Humanity has often wept over the fate of the aborigines of this country, and Philanthropy has been long busily employed in devising means to avert it, but its progress has never for a moment been arrested, and one by one have many powerful tribes disappeared from the earth. To follow to the tomb the last of his race and to tread on the graves of extinct nations excite melancholy reflections. But true philanthropy reconciles the mind to these vicissitudes as it does to the extinction of one generation to make room for another. In the monuments and fortifications of an unknown people, spread over the extensive regions of the West, we behold the memorials of a once powerful race, which was exterminated or has disappeared to make room for the existing savage tribes. Nor is there any thing in this which, upon a comprehensive view of the general interests of the human race, is to be regretted. Philanthropy could not wish to see this continent restored to the condition in which it was found by our forefathers. What good man would prefer a country covered with forests and ranged by a few thousand savages to our extensive Republic, studded with cities, towns, and prosperous farms, embellished with all the improvements which art can devise or industry execute, occupied by more than 12,000,000 happy people, and filled with all the blessings of liberty, civilization, and religion?

The present policy of the Government is but a continuation of the same progressive change by a milder process. The tribes which occupied the countries now constituting the Eastern States were annihilated or have melted away to make room for the whites. The waves of population and civilization are rolling to the westward, and we now propose to acquire the countries occupied by the red men of the South and West by a fair exchange, and, at the expense of the United States, to send them to a land where their existence may be prolonged and perhaps made perpetual.

Doubtless it will be painful to leave the graves of their fathers; but what do they more than our ancestors did or than our children are now doing? To better their condition in an unknown land our forefathers left all that was dear in earthly objects. Our children by thousands yearly leave the land of their birth to seek new homes in distant regions. Does Humanity weep at these painful separations from every thing, animate and inanimate, with which the young heart has become entwined? Far from it. It is rather a source of joy that our country affords scope where our young population may range unconstrained in body or in mind, developing the power and faculties of man in their highest perfection.

These remove hundreds and almost thousands of miles at their own expense, purchase the lands they occupy, and support themselves at their new homes from the moment of their arrival. Can it be cruel in this Government when, by events which it can not control, the Indian is made discontented in his ancient home to purchase his lands, to give him a new and extensive territory, to pay the expense of his removal, and support him a year in his new abode? How many thousands of our own people would gladly embrace the opportunity of removing to the West on such conditions! If the offers made to the Indians were extended to them, they would be hailed with gratitude and joy.

And is it supposed that the wandering savage has a stronger attachment to his home than the settled, civilized Christian? Is it more afflicting to him to leave the graves of his fathers than it is to our brothers and children? Rightly considered, the policy of the General Government toward the red man is not only liberal, but generous. He is unwilling to submit to the laws of the States and mingle with their population. To save him from this alternative, or perhaps utter annihilation, the General Government kindly offers him a new home, and proposes to pay the whole expense of his removal and settlement.

In the consummation of a policy originating at an early period, and steadily pursued by every Administration within the present century—so just to the States and so generous to the Indians—the Executive feels it has a right to expect the cooperation of Congress and of all good and disinterested men. The States, moreover, have a right to demand it. It was substantially a part of the compact which made them members of our Confederacy. With Georgia there is an express contract; with the new States an implied one of equal obligation. Why, in authorizing Ohio, Indiana, Illinois, Missouri, Mississippi, and Alabama to form constitutions and become separate States, did Congress include within their limits extensive tracts of Indian lands, and, in some instances, powerful Indian tribes? Was it not understood by both parties that the power of the States was to be coextensive with their limits, and that with all convenient dispatch the General Government should extinguish the Indian title and remove every obstruction to the complete jurisdiction of the State governments over the soil? Probably not one of those States would have accepted a separate existence—certainly it would never have been granted by Congress—had it been understood that they were to be confined for ever to those small portions of their nominal territory the Indian title to which had at the time been extinguished.

It is, therefore, a duty which this Government owes to the new States to extinguish as soon as possible the Indian title to all lands which Congress themselves have included within their limits. When this is done the duties of the General Government in relation to the States and the Indians within their limits are at an end. The Indians may leave the State or not, as they choose. The purchase of their lands does not alter in the least their personal relations with the State government. No act of the General Government has ever been deemed necessary to give the States jurisdiction over the persons of the Indians. That they possess by virtue of their sovereign power within their own limits in as full a manner before as after the purchase of the Indian lands; nor can this Government add to or diminish it.

May we not hope, therefore, that all good citizens, and none more zealously than those who think the Indians oppressed by subjection to the laws of the States, will unite in attempting to open the eyes of those children of the forest to their true condition, and by a speedy removal to relieve them from all the evils, real or imaginary, present or prospective, with which they may be supposed to be threatened.

Document 4: Elias Boudinot's Editorials in *The Cherokee Phoenix*

As editor in chief of the first Cherokee newspaper, *The Cherokee Phoenix*, Elias Boudinot wrote his editorials for two distinct audiences: his home audience, the Cherokee people, and his distant audience, interested and sympathetic U.S. citizens. He hoped to influence the former to be involved in Cherokee affairs internally, and he hoped to influence the latter to support the Cherokees from the outside, through the U.S. political system. In his June 17, 1829, piece, Boudinot pointed out how President Jackson's support of the state of Georgia's attempt to extend its jurisdiction to Cherokee lands represented a departure from previous presidents' policies. Moreover, the rationale Georgia employed to defend its position could have been used earlier— the Cherokee Nation had not moved or changed its boundaries; what had changed was that Georgia now had a president willing to back up its claim. The November 12, 1831, editorial contrasted the promise of the civilization campaign, which encouraged Cherokees to acculturate, with the state of Georgia's actions, which betrayed no interest in the welfare of the Cherokees, in Boudinot's opinion, but rather a simple desire to obtain Cherokee property. (Source: History Lives, available at http://www.cerritos.edu/soliver/Student%20Activities/Trail%20of%20 Tears/web/boudinot.htm#_edn1 [accessed January 7, 2006]. Also cited in Elias Boudinot, *Cherokee Editor: The Writings of Elias Boudinot*, ed. Theda Perdue [Athens: University of Georgia Press, 1996], pp. 108– 109, 140–143.)

June 17, 1829

From the documents which we this day lay before our readers, there is not a doubt of the kind of policy, which the present administration of the General Government intends to pursue relative to the Indians. President Jackson has, as a neighboring editor remarks, "recognized the doctrine contended for by Georgia in its full extent." It is to be regretted that we were not undeceived long ago, while we were hunters and in our savage state. It appears now from the communication of the Secretary of War to the Cherokee Delegation, that the illustrious Washington, Jefferson, Madison and Monroe were only tantalizing us, when they encouraged us in the pursuit of agriculture and Government, and when they afforded us the protection of the United States, by which we have been preserved to this present time as a nation. Why were we not told long ago, that we could not be permitted to establish a government within the limits of any state? Then we could have borne disappointment much easier than now. The pretext for Georgia to extend her jurisdiction over the Cherokees has always existed. The Cherokees have always had a government of their own. Nothing, however, was said when we were governed by savage laws, when the abominable law of retaliation carried death in our midst, when it was a lawful act to shed the blood of a person charged with witchcraft, when a brother could kill a brother with impunity, or an innocent man suffer for an offending relative. At that time it might have been a matter of charity to have extended over us the mantle of Christian laws & regulations. But how happens it now, after being fostered by the U. States, and advised by great and good men to establish a government of regular law; when the aid and protection of the General Government have been pledged to us; when we, as dutiful "children" of the President, have followed his instructions and advice, and have established for our selves a government of regular law; when everything looks so promising around us, that a storm is raised by the extension of tyrannical and unchristian laws, which threatens to blast all our rising hopes and expectations?

There is, as would naturally be supposed, a great rejoicing in Georgia.

It is a time of "important news"—"gratifying intelligence"—"The Cherokee lands are to be obtained speedily." It is even reported that the Cherokees have come to the conclusion to sell, and move off to the west of the Mississippi—not so fast. We are yet at our homes, at our peaceful firesides, (except those contiguous to Sandtown, Carroll, &c.) attending to our farms and useful occupations.

We had concluded to give our readers fully our thoughts on the subject, which we, in the above remarks, have merely introduced, but upon reflection & remembering our promise, that we will be moderate, we have suppressed ourselves, and have withheld what we had intended should occupy our editorial column. We do not wish, by any means, unnecessarily to excite the minds of the Cherokees. To our home readers we submit the subject without any special comment. They will judge for themselves. To our distant readers, who may wish to know how we feel under present circumstances, we recommend the memorial, the leading article in our present number. We believe it justly contains the views of the nation.

November 12, 1831

It has been customary to charge the failure of attempts heretofore made to civilize and christianize the aborigines to the Indians themselves. Whence originated the common saying, "An Indian will still be an Indian."—Do what you will, he cannot be civilized—you cannot reclaim him from his wild habits—you may as well expect to change the spots of the Leopard as to effect any substantial renovation in his character—he is as the wild Turkey, which at "night-fall seeks the tallest forest tree for his roosting place." Such assertions, although inconsistent with the general course of providence and the history of nations, have nevertheless been believed and acted upon by many well meaning persons. Such persons do not sufficiently consider that causes, altogether different from those they have been in the habit of assigning, may have operated to frustrate the benevolent efforts made to reclaim the Indian. They do not, perhaps, think that as God has, of one blood, created all the nations of the earth, their circumstances, in a state of nature, must be somewhat the same, and therefore, in the history of mankind, we have no example upon which we can build the assertion, that it is impossible to civilize and christianize the Indian. On the contrary we have instances of nations, originally as ignorant and barbarous as the American natives, having risen from their degraded state to a high pitch of refinement—from the worst kind of paganism to the knowledge of the true God.

We have on more than one occasion remarked upon the difficulties which lie in the way of civilizing the Indians. Those difficulties have been fully developed in the history of the Cherokees within the last two years. They are such as no one can now mistake—their nature is fully revealed, and the source from whence they rise can no longer be a matter of doubt. They are not to be found in the "nature" of the Indians, which a man in high authority once said was as difficult to change as the Leopard his spots. It is not because they are, of all others, the most degraded and ignorant that they have not been brought to enjoy the blessings of a civilized life.—But it is because they have to contend with obstacles as numerous as they are peculiar.

With a commendable zeal the first Chief magistrate of the United States undertook to bring the Cherokees into the pale of civilization, by establishing friendly relations with them by treaties, and introducing the mechanic arts among them. He was indeed a "father" to them—They regarded him as such—They placed confidence in what he said, and well they might, for he was true to his promises. Of course the foundation for the improvement which the Cherokees have since made was laid under the patronage of that illustrious man. His successors followed his example and treated their "red children" as human beings, capable of improvement, and possessing rights derived from the source of all good, and guarantied by compacts as solemn as a great Republic could make. The attempts of those good men were attended with success, because they believed those attempts were feasible and acted accordingly.

Upon the same principle have acted those benevolent associations who have taken such a deep interest in the welfare of the Indians, and who may have expended so much time and money in extending the benign influence of religion. Those associations went hand in hand with the Government—it was a work of co-operation. God blessed their efforts. The Cherokees have been reclaimed from their wild habits—Instead of hunters they have become the cultivators of the soil—Instead of wild and ferocious savages, thirsting for blood, they have become the mild "citizens," the friends and brothers of the white man—Instead of the superstitious heathens, many of them have become the worshippers of the true God. Well would it have been if the cheering fruits of those labors had been fostered and encouraged by an enlightened community! But alas! no sooner was it made manifest that the Cherokees were becoming strongly attached to the ways and usages of civilized life, than was aroused the opposition of those from whom better things ought to have been expected. No sooner was it known that they had learned the proper use of the earth, and that they were now less likely to dispose of their lands for a mess of pottage, than they came in conflict with the cupidity and self-interest of those who ought to have been their benefactors— Then commenced a series of obstacles hard to over come, and difficulties intended as a stumbling block, and unthought of before. The "Great Father" of the "red man" has lent his influence to encourage those difficulties. The guardian has deprived his wards of their rights—The sacred obligations of treaties and laws have been disregarded—The promises of Washington and Jefferson have not been fulfilled. The policy of the United States on Indian affairs has taken a different direction, for no other reason than that the Cherokees have so far become civilized as to appreciate a regular form of Government. They are now deprived of rights they once enjoyed—A neighboring power is now permitted to extend its withering hand over them—Their own laws, intended to regulate their society, to encourage virtue and to suppress vice, must now be abolished, and civilized acts, passed for the purpose of expelling them, must be substituted.—Their intelligent citizens who have been instructed through the means employed by former administrations, and through the efforts of benevolent societies, must be abused and insulted, represented as avaricious, feeding upon the poverty of the common Indians—the hostility of all those who want the Indian lands must be directed against them. That the Cherokees may be kept in ignorance, teachers who had settled among them by the approbation of the Government, for the best of all purposes, have been compelled to leave them by reason of laws unbecoming any civilized nation—Ministers of the Gospel, who might have, at this day of trial, administered to them the consolations of Religion, have been arrested, chained, dragged away before their eyes, tried as felons, and finally immured in prison with thieves and robbers.

Is not here an array of difficulties?—The truth is, while a portion of the community have been, in the most laudable manner, engaged in using efforts to civilize and christianize the Indian, another portion of the same community have been busy in counteracting those efforts. Cupidity and self-interest are at the bottom of all these difficulties—a desire to possess the Indian land is paramount to a desire to see him established on the soil as a civilized man.

Document 5: *Worcester v. Georgia,* March 1832

The *Worcester v. Georgia* decision was the second Chief Justice John Marshall made in cases regarding the Cherokee Nation. He had been sympathetic to the Cherokee plight during the *Cherokee Nation v. Georgia* case, although he did not find that the Cherokee Nation constituted a foreign country, as the Cherokees had hoped. *Worcester v. Georgia* took its name from Samuel Worcester, the missionary friend of Elias Boudinot, who was sentenced to hard labor for refusing to seek a Georgia permit to continue living and working among the Cherokees. Marshall agreed with the Cherokees that the state of Georgia had no jurisdiction over the Cherokee Nation. The decision declared Georgia's laws with relation to the Cherokee Nation unconstitutional and void. Marshall clearly explained that, according to the U.S. Constitution, it was the national government and not state governments that had the right to interact with and make agreements with the Cherokee Nation and other native nations. This contradicted Jackson's claim that the situation between Georgia and the Cherokees was a state matter. The decision was an empty victory, however, because both Georgia and President Jackson ignored it. (Source: *Worcester v. Georgia*, 31 U.S. 515 [1831], available at http://caselaw.lp.findlaw.com/scripts/getcase.pl?court=US&vol=31&invol=515 [accessed November 19, 2005].)

Mr. Chief Justice Marshall delivered the opinion of the Court.

Be it enacted by the Senate and House of Representatives of the State of Georgia in general assembly met, and it is hereby enacted by the authority of the same, that, after the 1st day of February 1831, it shall not be lawful for any person or persons, under colour or pretence of authority from said Cherokee tribe, or as headmen, chiefs or warriors of said tribe, to cause or procure by any means the assembling of any council or other pretended legislative body of the said Indians or others living among them, for the purpose of legislating (or for any other purpose whatever). And persons offending against the provisions of this section shall be guilty of a high misdemeanour, and subject to indictment therefor, and, on conviction, shall be punished by confinement at hard labour in the penitentiary for the space of four years.

Section 2. And be it further enacted by the authority aforesaid, that, after the time aforesaid, it shall not be lawful for any person or persons, under pretext of authority from the Cherokee tribe, or as representatives, chiefs, headmen or warriors of said tribe, to meet or assemble as a council, assembly, convention, or in any other capacity, for the purpose of making laws, orders or regulations for said tribe. And all persons offending against the provisions of this section shall be guilty of a high misdemeanour, and subject to an indictment, and, on conviction thereof, shall undergo an imprisonment in the penitentiary at hard labour for the space of four years.

Section 3. And be it further enacted by the authority aforesaid, that, after the time aforesaid, it shall not be lawful for any person or persons, under colour or by authority of the Cherokee tribe, or any of its laws or regulations, to hold any court or tribunal whatever for the purpose of hearing and determining causes, either civil or criminal, or to give any judgment in such causes, or to issue, or cause to issue, any process against the person or property of any of said tribe. And all persons offending against the provisions of this section shall be guilty of a high misdemeanour, and subject to indictment, and, on conviction thereof, shall be imprisoned in the penitentiary at hard labour for the space of four years.

Section 4. And be it further enacted by the authority aforesaid that, after the time aforesaid, it shall not be lawful for any person or persons, as a ministerial officer, or in any other capacity, to execute any precept, command or process issued by any court or tribunal in the Cherokee tribe, on the persons or property of any of said tribe. And all persons offending against the provisions of this section shall be guilty of a trespass, and subject to indictment, and, on conviction thereof, shall be punished by fine and imprisonment in the jail or in the penitentiary, not longer than four years, at the discretion of the court.

Section 5. And be it further enacted by the authority aforesaid that, after the time aforesaid, it shall not be lawful for any person or persons to confiscate, or attempt to confiscate, or otherwise to cause a forfeiture of the property or estate of any Indian of said tribe in consequence of his enrolling himself and family for emigration, or offering to enroll for emigration, or any other act of said Indian in furtherance of his intention to emigrate. And persons offending against the provisions of this section shall be guilty of high misdemeanour, and, on conviction, shall undergo an imprisonment in the penitentiary at hard labour for the space of four years.

Section 6. And be it further enacted by the authority aforesaid that none of the provisions of this act shall be so construed as to prevent said tribe, its headmen, chiefs or other representatives, from meeting any agent or commissioner on the part of this State or the United States for any purpose whatever.

Section 7. And be it further enacted by the authority aforesaid that all white persons residing within the limits of the Cherokee Nation, on the 1st day of March next, or at any time thereafter, without a license or permit from his Excellency the Governor, or from such agent as his Excellency the Governor shall authorise to grant such permit or license, and who shall not have taken the oath hereinafter required, shall be guilty of a high misdemeanour, and, upon conviction thereof, shall be punished by confinement to the penitentiary at hard labour for a term not less than four years: provided, that the provisions of this section shall not be so construed as to extend to any authorised agent or agents of the Government of the United States or of this State, or to any person or persons who may rent any of those improvements which have been abandoned by Indians who have emigrated west of the Mississippi; provided, nothing contained in this section shall be so construed as to extend to white females, and all male children under twenty-one years of age.

Section 8. And be it further enacted by the authority aforesaid, that all white persons, citizens of the State of Georgia, who have procured a license in writing from his Excellency the Governor, or from such agent as his Excellency the Governor shall authorise to grant such permit or license, to reside within the limits of the Cherokee Nation, and who have taken the following oath, viz., "I, A.B., do solemnly swear (or affirm, as the case may be) that I will support and defend the Constitution and laws of the State of Georgia, and uprightly demean myself as a citizen thereof, so help me God," shall be, and the same are hereby declared exempt and free from the operation of the seventh section of this act.

Section 9. And be it further enacted that his Excellency the Governor be, and he is hereby, authorized to grant licenses to reside within the limits of the Cherokee Nation, according to the provisions of the eighth section of this act.

Section 10. And be it further enacted by the authority aforesaid that no person shall collect or claim any toll from any person for passing any turnpike gate or toll bridge by authority of any act or law of the Cherokee tribe, or any chief or headman or men of the same.

Section 11. And be it further enacted by the authority aforesaid that his Excellency the Governor be, and he is hereby, empowered, should he deem it necessary, either for the protection of the mines or for the enforcement of the laws of force within the Cherokee Nation, to raise and organize a guard, to be employed on foot, or mounted, as occasion may require, which shall not consist of more than sixty persons, which guard shall be under the command of the commissioner or agent appointed by the Governor, to protect the mines, with power to dismiss from the service any member of said guard, on paying the wages due for services rendered, for disorderly conduct, and make appointments to fill the vacancies occasioned by such dismissal.

Section 12. And be it further enacted by the authority aforesaid, that each person who may belong to said guard, shall receive for his compensation at the rate of fifteen dollars per month when on foot, and at the rate of twenty dollars per month when mounted, for every month that such person is engaged in actual service; and, in the event, that the commissioner or agent, herein referred to, should die, resign, or fail to perform the duties herein required of him, his Excellency the Governor is hereby authorised and required to appoint, in his stead, some other fit and proper person to the command of said guard; and the commissioner or agent, having the command of the guard aforesaid, for the better discipline thereof, shall appoint three sergeants, who shall receive at the rate of twenty dollars per month while serving on foot, and twenty-five dollars per month, when mounted, as compensation whilst in actual service.

Section 13. And be it further enacted by the authority aforesaid that the said guard, or any member of them, shall be, and they are hereby, authorised and empowered to arrest any person legally charged with, or detected in, a violation of the laws of this State, and to convey, as soon as practicable, the person so arrested before a justice of the peace, judge of the superior or justice of inferior court of this State, to be dealt with according to law; and the pay and support of said guard be provided out of the fund already appropriated for the protection of the gold mines.

The legislature of Georgia, on the 19th December 1829, passed the following act:

An act to add the territory lying within the chartered limits of Georgia, and now in the occupancy of the Cherokee Indians, to the counties of Carroll, De Kalb, Gwinnett, Hall, and Habersham, and to extend the laws of this State over the same, and to annul all laws and ordinances made by the Cherokee Nation of Indians, and to provide for the compensation of officers serving legal process in said territory, and to regulate the testimony of Indians, and to repeal the ninth section of the act of 1828 upon this subject.

Section 1. Be it enacted by the senate and house of representatives of the State of Georgia in general assembly met, and it is hereby enacted by the authority of the same, that, from and after the passing of this Act, all that part of the unlocated territory within the limits of this State, and which lies between the Alabama line and the old path leading from the Buzzard Roost on the Chattahoochee, to Sally Hughes', on the Hightower River; thence to Thomas Pelet's on the old federal road; thence with said road to the Alabama line be, and the same is hereby added to, and shall become a part of, the County of Carroll.

Section 2. And be it further enacted that all that part of said territory lying and being north of the last mentioned line and south of the road running from Charles Gait's ferry, on the Chattahoochee River, to Dick Roe's, to where it intersects with the path aforesaid, be, and the same is hereby added to, and shall become a part of, the County of De Kalb.

Section 3. And be it further enacted, that all that part of the said territory lying north of the last mentioned line and south of a line commencing at the mouth of Baldridge's Creek; thence up said creek to its source; from thence to where the federal road crosses the Hightower; thence with said road to the Tennessee line, be, and the same is hereby added to, and shall become part of, the County of Gwinnett.

Section 4. And be it further enacted that all that part of the said territory lying north of said last mentioned line and south [p*526] of a line to commence on the Chestatee River, at the mouth of Yoholo Creek; thence up said creek to the top of the Blue ridge; thence to the head waters of Notley River; thence down said river to the boundary line of Georgia, be, and the same is hereby added to, and shall become a part of, the County of Hall.

Section 5. And be it further enacted that all that part of said territory lying north of said last mentioned line, within the limits of this State, be, and the same is hereby added to, and shall become a part of, the County of Habersham.

Section 6. And be it further enacted, that all the laws, both civil and criminal, of this State, be, and the same are hereby, extended over said portions of territory, respectively; and all persons whatever, residing within the same, shall, after the 1st day of June next, be subject and liable to the operation of said laws in the same manner as other citizens of this State, or the citizens of said counties, respectively, and all writs and processes whatever, issued by the courts or officers of said courts, shall extend over, and operate on, the portions of territory hereby added to the same, respectively.

Section 7. And be it further enacted that, after the 1st day of June next, all laws, ordinances, orders and regulations, of any kind whatever, made, passed or enacted, by the Cherokee Indians, either in general council or in any other way whatever, or by any authority whatever of said tribe, be, and the same are hereby declared to be, null and void, and of no effect, as if the same had never existed, and, in all cases of indictment or civil suits, it shall not be lawful for the defendant to justify under any of said laws, ordinances, orders or regulations; nor shall the courts of this State permit the same to be given in evidence on the trial of any suit whatever.

Section 8. And be it further enacted that it shall not be lawful for any person or body of persons, by arbitrary power or by virtue of any pretended rule, ordinance, law or custom of said Cherokee Nation, to prevent by threats, menaces or other means, or endeavour to prevent, any Indian of said Nation residing within the chartered limits of this State, from enrolling as an emigrant, or actually emigrating or removing from said nation; nor shall it be lawful for any person or body of persons, by arbitrary power or by virtue of any pretended rule, ordinance, law or custom of said nation, to punish, in any manner, or to molest either the person or property, or to abridge the rights or privileges of any Indian, for enrolling his or her name as an emigrant, or for emigrating or intending to emigrate, from said nation.

Section 9. And be it further enacted that any person or body of persons offending against the provisions of the foregoing section shall be guilty of a high misdemeanour, subject to indictment, and on conviction shall be punished by confinement in the common jail of any county of this State, or by confinement at hard labour in the penitentiary, for a term not exceeding four years, at the discretion of the court.

Section 10. And be it further enacted that it shall not be lawful for any person or body of persons, by arbitrary power, or under colour of any pretended rule, ordinance, law or custom of said nation, to prevent or offer to prevent, or deter any Indian headman, chief or warrior of said nation, residing within the chartered limits of this State, from selling or ceding to the United States, for the use of Georgia, the whole or any part of said territory, or to prevent or offer to prevent, any Indian, headman, chief or warrior of said nation, residing as aforesaid, from meeting in council or treaty any commissioner or commissioners on the part of the United States, for any purpose whatever.

Section 11. And be it further enacted, that any person or body of persons offending against the provisions of the foregoing sections, shall be guilty of a high misdemeanour, subject to indictment, and on conviction shall be confined at hard labour in the penitentiary for not less than four nor longer than six years, at the discretion of the court.

Section 12. And be it further enacted, that it shall not be lawful for any person or body of persons, by arbitrary force, or under colour of any pretended rules, ordinances, law or custom of said nation, to take the life of any Indian residing as aforesaid, for enlisting as an emigrant, attempting to emigrate, ceding, or attempting to cede, as aforesaid, the whole or any part of the said territory, or meeting or attempting to meet, in treaty or in council, as aforesaid, any commissioner or commissioners aforesaid; and any person or body of persons offending against the provisions of this section shall be guilty of murder, subject to indictment, and, on conviction, shall suffer death by hanging.

Section 13. And be it further enacted that, should any of the foregoing offences be committed under colour of any pretended rules, ordinances, custom or law of said nation, all persons acting therein, either as individuals or as pretended executive, ministerial or judicial officers, shall be deemed and considered as principals, and subject to the pains and penalties herein before described.

Section 14. And be it further enacted that for all demands which may come within the jurisdiction of a magistrate's court, suit may be brought for the same in the nearest district of the county to which the territory is hereby annexed, and all officers serving any legal process on any person living on any portion of the territory herein named shall be entitled to recover the sum of five cents for every mile he may ride to serve the same, after crossing the present limits of the said counties, in addition to the fees already allowed by law; and in case any of the said officers should be resisted in the execution of any legal process issued by any court or magistrate, justice of the inferior court, or judge of the superior court of any of said counties, he is hereby authorised to call out a sufficient number of the militia of said counties to aid and protect him in the execution of this duty.

Section 15. And be it further enacted that no Indian or descendant of any Indian residing within the Creek or Cherokee Nations of Indians shall be deemed a competent witness in any court of this State to which a white person may be a party, except such white person resides within the said nation.

In September 1831, the grand jurors for the county of Gwinnett in the State of Georgia, presented to the superior court of the county the following indictment:

Georgia, Gwinnett county: The grand jurors, sworn, chosen and selected for the county of Gwinnett, in the name and behalf of the citizens of Georgia, charge and accuse Elizur Butler, Samuel A. Worcester, James Trott, Samuel Mays, Surry Eaton, Austin Copeland, and Edward D. Losure, white persons of said county, with the offence of "residing within the limits of the Cherokee Nation without a license:" For that the said Elizur Butler, Samuel A. Worcester, James Trott, Samuel Mays, Surry Eaton, Austin

Copeland and Edward D. Losure, white persons, as aforesaid, on the 15th day of July 1831, did reside in that part of the Cherokee Nation attached by the laws of said State to the said county, and in the county aforesaid, without a license or permit from his Excellency the Governor of said State, or from any agent authorised by his Excellency the Governor aforesaid to grant such permit or license, and without having taken the oath to support and defend the Constitution and laws of the State of Georgia, and uprightly to demean themselves as citizens thereof, contrary to the laws of said State, the good order, peace and dignity thereof.

To this indictment, the plaintiff in error pleaded specially, as follows:

And the said Samuel A. Worcester, in his own proper person, comes and says that this Court ought not to take further cognizance of the action and prosecution aforesaid, because, he says, that on the 15th day of July in the year 1831, he was, and still is, a resident in the Cherokee Nation, and that the said supposed crime, or crimes, and each of them, were committed, if committee at all, at the town of New Echota, in the said Cherokee Nation, out of the jurisdiction of this Court, and not in the county Gwinnett, or elsewhere within the jurisdiction of this Court. And this defendant saith, that he is a citizen of the State of Vermont, one of the United States of America, and that he entered the aforesaid Cherokee Nation in the capacity of a duly authorised missionary of the American Board of Commissioners for Foreign Missions, under the authority of the President of the United States, and has not since been required by him to leave it; that he was, at the time of his arrest, engaged in preaching the gospel to the Cherokee Indians, and in translating the sacred Scriptures into their language, with the permission and approval of the said Cherokee Nation, and in accordance with the humane policy of the Government of the United States, for the civilization and improvement of the Indians, and that his residence there, for this purpose, is the residence charged in the aforesaid indictment, and this defendant further saith that this prosecution the State of Georgia ought not to have or maintain, because he saith that several treaties have, from time to time, been entered into between the United States and the Cherokee Nation of Indians, to-wit, at Hopewell on the 28th day of November, 1785; at Holston on the 2d day of July, 1791; at Philadelphia on the 26th day of June, 1794; at Tellico on the 2d day of October, 1798; at Tellico on the 24th day of October, 1804; at Tellico on the 25th day of October, 1805; at Tellico on the 27th day of October, 1805; at Washington City on the 7th day of January, 1805; at Washington City on the 22d day of March, 1816; at the Chickasaw Council House on the 14th day of September, 1816; at the Cherokee Agency on the 8th day of July, 1817, and at Washington City on the 27th day of February, 1819, all which treaties have been duly ratified by the Senate of the United States of America, and by which treaties the United States of America acknowledge the said Cherokee Nation to be a sovereign nation, authorised to govern themselves, and all persons who have settled within their territory, free from any right of legislative interference by the several states composing the United States of America in reference to acts done within their own territory, and by which treaties the whole of the territory now occupied by the Cherokee Nation on the east of the Mississippi has been solemnly guarantied to them, all of which treaties are existing treaties at this day, and in full force. By these treaties, and particularly by the treaties of Hopewell and Holston, the aforesaid territory is acknowledged to lie without the jurisdiction of the several states composing the Union of the United States; and, it is thereby specially stipulated that the citizens of the United States shall not enter the aforesaid territory, even on a visit, without a passport from the Governor of a State, or from some one duly authorised thereto by the President of the United States, all of which will more fully and at large appear by reference to the aforesaid treaties. And this defendant saith that the several acts charged in the bill of indictment were done or omitted to be done, if at all, within the said territory so recognized as belonging to the said Nation, and so, as aforesaid, held by them, under the guarantee of the United States; that for those acts the defendant is not amenable to the laws of Georgia, nor to the jurisdiction of the courts of the said State; and that the laws of the State of Georgia, which profess to add the said territory to the several adjacent counties of the said State, and to extend the laws of Georgia over the said territory and persons inhabiting the same, and, in particular, the act on which this indictment against this defendant is grounded, to-wit:

An act entitled an act to prevent the exercise of assumed and arbitrary power by all persons, under pretext of authority from the Cherokee Indians, and their laws, and to prevent white persons from residing within that part of the chartered limits of Georgia occupied by the Cherokee Indians, and to provide a guard for the protection of the gold mines, and to enforce the laws of the State within the aforesaid territory, are repugnant to the aforesaid treaties, which, according to the Constitution of the United States, compose a part of the supreme law of the land, and that these laws of Georgia are therefore unconstitutional, void, and of no effect; that the said laws of Georgia are also unconstitutional and void because they impair the obligation of the various contracts formed by and between the aforesaid Cherokee Nation and the said United States of America, as above recited; also that the said laws of Georgia are unconstitutional and void because they interfere with, and attempt to regulate and control, the intercourse with the said Cherokee Nation, which, by the said Constitution, belongs exclusively to the Congress of the United States; and because the said laws are repugnant to the statute of the United States, passed on ___ day of March 1802, entitled "an act to regulate trade and intercourse with the Indian tribes, and to preserve peace on the frontiers;" and that, therefore, this Court has no jurisdiction to cause this defendant to make further or other answer to the said bill of indictment, or further to try and punish this defendant for the said supposed offence or offences alleged in the bill of indictment, or any of them; and therefore this defendant prays judgment whether he shall be held bound to answer further to said indictment.

This plea was overruled by the court; and the jurisdiction of the Superior Court of the County of Gwinnett was sustained by the judgment of the court.

The defendant was then arraigned, and pleaded "not guilty," and the case came on for trial on the 15th of September 1831, when the jury found the defendants in the indictment guilty. On the same day the court pronounced sentence on the parties so convicted, as follows:

The State v. B. F. Thompson and others. Indictment for residing in the Cherokee Nation without license. Verdict, Guilty.

The State v. Elizur Butler, Samuel A. Worcester and others. Indictment for residing in the Cherokee Nation without license. Verdict, Guilty.

The defendants in both of the above cases shall be kept in close custody by the sheriff of this county until they can be transported to the penitentiary of this State, and the keeper thereof is hereby directed to receive them, and each of them, into his custody, and keep them, and each of them, at hard labour in said penitentiary, for and during the term of four years.

A writ of error was issued on the application of the plaintiff in error, on the 27th of October 1831, which, with the following proceedings thereon, was returned to this court.

United States of America, The President of the United States to the honourable the judges of the Superior Court for the County of Gwinnett, in the State of Georgia, greeting:

Because in the record and proceedings, as also in the rendition of the judgment of a plea which is in the said superior court, for the county of Gwinnett, before you, or some of you, between the State of Georgia, plaintiff, and Samuel A. Worcester, defendant, on an indictment, being the highest court of law in said State in which a decision could be had in said suit, a manifest error hath happened, to the great damage of the said Samuel A. Worcester, as by his complaint appears. We being willing that error, if any hath been, should be duly corrected, and full and speedy justice done to the parties aforesaid in this behalf, do command you, if judgment be therein given that then under

your seal distinctly and openly, you send the record and proceedings aforesaid, with all things concerning the same, to the
Supreme Court of the United States, together with this writ, so
that you have the same at Washington on the second Monday of
January next, in the said Supreme Court, to be then and there
held; that the record and proceedings aforesaid being inspected,
the said Supreme Court may cause further to be done therein, to
correct that error, what of right, and according to the laws and
custom of the United States, should be done.

Witness, the honourable John Marshall, chief justice of the
said Supreme Court, the first Monday of August in the year of
our Lord one thousand eight hundred and thirty-one.

Document 6: Treaty of New Echota, Signed December 29, 1835 (Proclaimed May 23, 1836)

Although the Cherokee signers of the Treaty of New Echota
believed they were choosing the only option that would allow for
the survival of the Cherokee Nation, most Cherokees blamed them
and the treaty for the Trail of Tears. Members of the Treaty Party, led
by Major Ridge, John Ridge, and Elias Boudinot, had no legal
authority to represent the Cherokee Nation when they signed the
Treaty of New Echota, agreeing to a removal offer made by the U.S.
government that had been rejected previously by the Cherokee
National Council. Passage of the treaty required an affirmative vote
of two-thirds of the U.S. senators present. On May 18, 1838, the
treaty passed by one vote, 31 to 15. Those opposed to the treaty
included Senators Henry Clay from Kentucky and Daniel Webster
from Massachusetts; Congressman and former President John Quincy
Adams also voiced strong disapproval of the treaty. The strongest
support for the treaty, besides that from Andrew Jackson, came from
Senators Alfred Cuthbert and John Pendleton King of Georgia and
Hugh Lawson White and Felix Grundy of Tennessee. The treaty provided for two years during which the Cherokees could relocate; the
physical removal of the Cherokees by force began two years to the
day after the treaty was proclaimed. (Source: *Indian Affairs: Laws and
Treaties*, vol. 2, *Treaties*, ed. Charles J. Kappler [Washington, DC:
Government Printing Office, 1904], pp. 439–449.)

*Articles of a treaty, concluded at New Echota in the State of Georgia
on the 29th day of Decr. 1835 by General William Carroll and John
F. Schermerhorn commissioners on the part of the United States and
the Chiefs Head Men and People of the Cherokee tribe of Indians.*

Whereas the Cherokees are anxious to make some arrangements with the Government of the United States whereby the difficulties they have experienced by a residence within the settled parts of the United States under the jurisdiction and laws of the State Governments may be terminated and adjusted; and with a view to reuniting their people in one body and securing a permanent home for themselves and their posterity in the country selected by their forefathers without the territorial limits of the State sovereignties, and where they can establish and enjoy a government of their choice and perpetuate such a state of society as may be most consonant with their views, habits and condition; and as may tend to their individual comfort and their advancement in civilization.

And whereas a delegation of the Cherokee nation composed of Messrs. John Ross Richard Taylor Danl. McCoy Samuel Gunter and William Rogers with full power and authority to conclude a treaty with the United States did on the 28th day of February 1835 stipulate and agree with the Government of the United States to submit to the Senate to fix the amount which should be allowed the Cherokees for their claims and for a cession of their lands east of the Mississippi river, and did agree to abide by the award of the Senate of the United States themselves and to recommend the same to their people for their final determination.

And whereas on such submission the Senate advised "that a sum not exceeding five millions of dollars be paid to the Cherokee Indians for all their lands and possessions east of the Mississippi river."

And whereas this delegation after said award of the Senate had been made, were called upon to submit propositions as to its disposition to be arranged in a treaty which they refused to do, but insisted that the same "should be referred to their nation and there in general council to deliberate and determine on the subject in order to ensure harmony and good feeling among themselves."

And whereas a certain other delegation composed of John Ridge Elias Boudinot Archilla Smith S. W. Bell John West Wm. A. Davis and Ezekiel West, who represented that portion of the nation in favor of emigration to the Cherokee country west of the Mississippi entered into propositions for a treaty with John F. Schermerhorn commissioner on the part of the United States which were to be submitted to their nation for their final action and determination:

And whereas the Cherokee people at their last October council at Red Clay, fully authorized and empowered a delegation or committee of twenty persons of their nation to enter into and conclude a treaty with the United States commissioner then present, *at that place or elsewhere* and as the people had good reason to believe that a treaty would then and there be made or at a subsequent council at New Echota which the commissioners it was well known and understood, were authorized and instructed to convene for said purpose; and since the said delegation have gone on to Washington city, with a view to close negotiations there, as stated by them notwithstanding they were officially informed by the United States commissioner that they would not be received by the President of the United States; and that the Government would transact no business of this nature with them, and that if a treaty was made it must be done here in the nation, where the delegation at Washington last winter *urged that it should be done for the purpose of promoting peace and harmony among the people*; and since these facts have also been corroborated to us by a communication recently received by the commissioner from the Government of the United States and read and explained to the people in open council and therefore believing said delegation can effect nothing and since our difficulties are daily increasing and our situation is rendered more and more precarious uncertain and insecure in consequence of the legislation of the States; and seeing no effectual way of relief, but in accepting the liberal overtures of the United States.

And whereas Genl William Carroll and John F. Schermerhorn were appointed commissioners on the part of the United States, with full power and authority to conclude a treaty with the Cherokees east and were directed by the President to convene the people of the nation in general council at New Echota and to submit said propositions to them with power and authority to vary the same so as to meet the views of the Cherokees in reference to its details.

And whereas the said commissioners did appoint and notify a general council of the nation to convene at New Echota on the 21st day of December 1835; and informed them that the commissioners would be prepared to make a treaty with the Cherokee people who should assemble there and those who did not come they should conclude gave their assent and sanction to whatever should be transacted at this council and the people having met in council according to said notice.

Therefore the following articles of a treaty are agreed upon and concluded between William Carroll and John F. Schermerhorn commissioners on the part of the United States and the chiefs and head men and people of the Cherokee nation in general council assembled this 29th day of Decr 1835.

ARTICLE 1. The Cherokee nation hereby cede relinquish and convey to the United States all the lands owned claimed or possessed by them east of the Mississippi river, and hereby release all their claims upon the United States for spoliations of every kind for and in consideration of the sum of five millions of dollars to be expended paid and invested in the manner stipulated and agreed upon in the following articles But as a question has arisen between the commissioners and the Cherokees whether the Senate in their resolution by which they advised "that a sum not exceeding five millions of dollars be paid to the Cherokee Indians for all their lands and possessions east of the Mississippi river" have included and made any allowance or consideration for claims for spoliations it is therefore agreed on the part of the United States that this question shall be again submitted to the Senate for their consideration and decision and if no allowance was made for spoliations that then an additional sum of three hundred thousand dollars be allowed for the same.

ARTICLE 2. Whereas by the treaty of May 6th 1828 and the supplementary treaty thereto of Feb. 14th 1833 with the Cherokees west of the Mississippi the United States guarantied and secured to be conveyed by patent, to the Cherokee nation of Indians the following tract of country "Beginning at a point on the old western territorial line of Arkansas Territory being twenty-five miles north from the point where the territorial line crosses Arkansas river, thence running from said north point south on the said territorial line where the said territorial line crosses Verdigris river; thence down said Verdigris river to the Arkansas river; thence down said Arkansas to a point where a stone is placed opposite the east or lower bank of Grand river at its junction with the Arkansas; thence running south forty-four degrees west one mile; thence in a straight line to a point four miles northerly, from the mouth of the north fork of the Canadian; thence along the said four mile line to the Canadian; thence down the Canadian to the Arkansas; thence down the Arkansas to that point on the Arkansas where the eastern Choctaw boundary strikes said river and running thence with the western line of Arkansas Territory as now defined, to the southwest corner of Missouri; thence along the western Missouri line to the land assigned the Senecas; thence on the south line of the Senecas to Grand river; thence up said Grand river as far as the south line of the Osage reservation, extended if necessary; thence up and between said south Osage line extended west if necessary, and a line drawn due west from the point of beginning to a certain distance west, at which a line running north and south from said Osage line to said due west line will make seven millions of acres within the whole described boundaries. In addition to the seven millions of acres of land thus provided for and bounded, the United States further guaranty to the Cherokee nation a perpetual outlet west, and a free and unmolested use of all the country west of the western boundary of said seven millions of acres, as far west as the sovereignty of the United States and their right of soil extend:

Provided however That if the saline or salt plain on the western prairie shall fall within said limits prescribed for said outlet, the right is reserved to the United States to permit other tribes of red men to get salt on said plain in common with the Cherokees; And letters patent shall be issued by the United States as soon as practicable for the land hereby guarantied."

And whereas it is apprehended by the Cherokees that in the above cession there is not contained a sufficient quantity of land for the accommodation of the whole nation on their removal west of the Mississippi the United States in consideration of the sum of five hundred thousand dollars therefore hereby covenant and agree to convey to the said Indians, and their descendants by patent, in fee simple the following additional tract of land situated between the west line of the State of Missouri and the Osage reservation beginning at the southeast corner of the same and runs north along the east line of the Osage lands fifty miles to the northeast corner thereof; and thence east to the west line of the State of Missouri; thence with said line south fifty miles; thence west to the place of beginning; estimated to contain eight hundred thousand acres of land; but it is expressly understood that if any of the lands assigned the Quapaws shall fall within the aforesaid bounds the same shall be reserved and excepted out of the lands above granted and a pro rata reduction shall be made in the price to be allowed to the United States for the same by the Cherokees.

ARTICLE 3. The United States also agree that the lands above ceded by the treaty of Feb. 14 1833, including the outlet, and those ceded by this treaty shall all be included in one patent executed to the Cherokee nation of Indians by the President of the United States according to the provisions of the act of May 28 1830. It is, however, agreed that the military reservation at Fort Gibson shall be held by the United States. But should the United States abandon said post and have no further use for the same it shall revert to the Cherokee nation. The United States shall always have the right to make and establish such post and military roads and forts in any part of the Cherokee country, as they may deem proper for the interest and protection of the same and the free use of as much land, timber, fuel and materials of all kinds for the construction and support of the same as may be necessary; provided that if the private rights of individuals are interfered with, a just compensation therefor shall be made.

ARTICLE 4. The United States also stipulate and agree to extinguish for the benefit of the Cherokees the titles to the reservations within their country made in the Osage treaty of 1825 to certain half-breeds and for this purpose they hereby agree to pay to the persons to whom the same belong or have been assigned or to their agents or guardians whenever they shall execute after the ratification of this treaty a satisfactory conveyance for the same, to the United States, the sum of fifteen thousand dollars according to a schedule accompanying this treaty of the relative value of the several reservations.

And whereas by the several treaties between the United States and the Osage Indians the Union and Harmony Missionary reservations which were established for their benefit are now situated within the country ceded by them to the United States; the former being situated in the Cherokee country and the latter in the State of Missouri. It is therefore agreed that the United States shall pay the American Board of Commissioners for Foreign Missions for the improvements on the same what they shall be appraised at by Capt. Geo. Vashon Cherokee sub-agent Abraham Redfield and A. P. Chouteau or such persons as the President of the United States shall appoint and the money allowed for the same shall be expended in schools among the Osages and improving their condition. It is understood that the United States are to pay the amount allowed for the reservations in this article and not the Cherokees.

ARTICLE 5. The United States hereby covenant and agree that the lands ceded to the Cherokee nation in the forgoing article shall, in no future time without their consent, be included within the territorial limits or jurisdiction of any State or Territory. But they shall secure to the Cherokee nation the right by their national councils to make and carry into effect all such laws as they may deem necessary for the government and protection of the persons and property within their own country belonging to their people or such persons as have connected themselves with them: provided always that they shall not be inconsistent with the constitution of the United States and such acts of Congress as have been or may be passed regulating trade and intercourse with the Indians; and also, that they shall not be considered as extending to such citizens and army of the United States as may travel or reside in the Indian country by permission according to the laws and regulations established by the Government of the same.

ARTICLE 6. Perpetual peace and friendship shall exist between the citizens of the United States and the Cherokee Indians. The United States agree to protect the Cherokee nation from domestic strife and foreign enemies and against internecine wars between the several tribes. The Cherokees shall endeavor to preserve and maintain the peace of the country and not make war upon their neighbors they shall also be protected against interruption and intrusion from citizens of the United States, who may attempt to settle in the country without their consent; and all such persons shall be removed from the same by order of the President of the United States. But this is not intended to prevent the residence among them of useful farmers mechanics and teachers for the instruction of Indians according to treaty stipulations.

ARTICLE 7. The Cherokee nation having already made great progress in civilization and deeming it important that every proper and laudable inducement should be offered to their people to improve their condition as well as to guard and secure in the most effectual manner the rights guarantied to them in this treaty, and with a view to illustrate the liberal and enlarged policy of the Government of the United States towards the Indians in their removal beyond the territorial limits of the States, it is stipulated that they shall be entitled to a delegate in the House of Representatives of the United States whenever Congress shall make provision for the same.

ARTICLE 8. The United States also agree and stipulate to remove the Cherokees to their new homes and to subsist them one year after their arrival there and that a sufficient number of steamboats and baggage-wagons shall be furnished to remove them comfortably, and so as not to endanger their health, and that a physician well supplied with medicines shall accompany each detachment of emigrants removed by the Government. Such persons and families as in the opinion of the emigrating agent are capable of subsisting and removing themselves shall be permitted to do so; and they shall be allowed in full for all claims for the same twenty dollars for each member of their family; and in lieu of their one year's rations they shall be paid the sum of thirty-three dollars and thirty-three cents if they prefer it.

Such Cherokees also as reside at present out of the nation and shall remove with them in two years west of the Mississippi shall be entitled to allowance for removal and subsistence as above provided.

ARTICLE 9. The United States agree to appoint suitable agents who shall make a just and fair valuation of all such improvements now in the possession of the Cherokees as add any value to the lands; and also of the ferries owned by them, according to their net income; and such improvements and ferries from which they have been dispossessed in a lawless manner or under any existing laws of the State where the same may be situated.

The just debts of the Indians shall be paid out of any monies due them for their improvements and claims; and they shall also be furnished at the discretion of the President of the United States with a sufficient sum to enable them to obtain the necessary means to remove themselves to their new homes, and the balance of their dues shall be paid them at the Cherokee agency west of the Mississippi. The missionary establishments shall also be valued and appraised in a like manner and the amount of them paid over by the United States to the treasurers of the respective missionary societies by whom they have been established and improved in order to enable them to erect such buildings and make such improvements among the Cherokees west of the Mississippi as they may deem necessary for their benefit. Such teachers at present among the Cherokees as this council shall select and designate shall be removed west of the Mississippi with the Cherokee nation and on the same terms allowed to them.

ARTICLE 10. The President of the United States shall invest in some safe and most productive public stocks of the country for the benefit of the whole Cherokee nation who have removed or shall remove to the lands assigned by this treaty to the Cherokee nation west of the Mississippi the following sums as a permanent fund for the purposes hereinafter specified and pay over the net income of the same annually to such person or persons as shall be authorized or appointed by the Cherokee nation to receive the same and their receipt shall be a full discharge for the amount paid to them viz: the sum of two hundred thousand dollars in addition to the present annuities of the nation to constitute a general fund the interest of which shall be applied annually by the council of the nation to such purposes as they may deem best for the general interest of their people. The sum of fifty thousand dollars to constitute an orphans' fund the annual income of which shall be expended towards the support and education of such orphan children as are destitute of the means of subsistence. The sum of one hundred and fifty thousand dollars in addition to the present school fund of the nation shall constitute a permanent school fund, the interest of which shall be applied annually by the council of the nation for the support of common schools and such a literary institution of a higher order as may be established in the Indian country. And in order to secure as far as possible the true and beneficial application of the orphans' and school fund the council of the Cherokee nation when required by the President of the United States shall make a report of the application of those funds and he shall at all times have the right if the funds have been misapplied to correct any abuses of them and direct the manner of their application for the purposes for which they were intended. The council of the nation may by giving two years' notice of their intention withdraw their funds by and with the consent of the President and Senate of the United States, and invest them in such manner as they may deem most proper for their interest. The United States also agree and stipulate to pay the just debts and claims against the Cherokee nation held by the citizens of the same and also the just claims of citizens of the United States for services rendered to the nation and the sum of sixty thousand dollars is appropriated for this purpose but no claims against individual persons of the nation shall be allowed and paid by the nation. The sum of three hundred thousand dollars is hereby set apart to pay and liquidate the just claims of the Cherokees upon the United States for spoliations of every kind, that have not been already satisfied under former treaties.

ARTICLE 11. The Cherokee nation of Indians believing it will be for the interest of their people to have all their funds and annuities under their own direction and future disposition hereby agree to commute their permanent annuity of ten thousand dollars for the sum of two hundred and fourteen thousand dollars, the same to be invested by the President of the United States as a part of the general fund of the nation; and their present school fund amounting to about fifty thousand dollars shall constitute a part of the permanent school fund of the nation.

ARTICLE 12. Those individuals and families of the Cherokee nation that are averse to a removal to the Cherokee country west of the Mississippi and are desirous to become citizens of the States where they reside and such as are qualified to take care of themselves and their property shall be entitled to receive their due portion of all the personal benefits accruing under this treaty for their claims, improvements and *per capita*; as soon as an appropriation is made for this treaty.

Such heads of Cherokee families as are desirous to reside within the States of No. Carolina, Tennessee, and Alabama subject to the laws of the same; and who are qualified or calculated to become useful citizens shall be entitled, on the certificate of the commissioners to a preemption right to one hundred and sixty acres of land or one quarter section at the minimum Congress price; so as to include the present buildings or improvements of those who now reside there and such as do not live there at present shall be permitted to locate within two years any lands not already occupied by persons entitled to pre-emption privilege under this treaty and if two or more families live on the same quarter section and they desire to continue their residence in these States and are qualified as above specified they shall, on receiving their pre-emption certificate be entitled to the right of pre-emption to such lands as they may select not already taken by any person entitled to them under this treaty.

It is stipulated and agreed between the United States and the Cherokee people that John Ross, James Starr, George Hicks, John Gunter, George Chambers, John Ridge, Elias Boudinot, George Sanders, John Martin, William Rogers, Roman Nose Situwake, and John Timpson shall be a committee on the part of the Cherokees to recommend such persons for the privilege of pre-emption rights as may be deemed entitled to the same under the above articles and to select the missionaries who shall be removed with the nation; and that they be hereby fully empowered and authorized to transact all business on the part of the Indians which may arise in carrying into effect the provisions of this treaty and settling the same with the United States. If any of the persons above mentioned should decline acting or be removed by death; the vacancies shall be filled by the committee themselves.

It is also understood and agreed that the sum of one hundred thousand dollars shall be expended by the commissioners in such manner as the committee deem best for the benefit of the poorer class of Cherokees as shall remove west or have removed west and are entitled to the benefits of this treaty. The same to be delivered at the Cherokee agency west as soon after the removal of the nation as possible.

ARTICLE 13. In order to make a final settlement of all the claims of the Cherokees for reservations granted under former treaties to any individuals belonging to the nation by the United States it is therefore hereby stipulated and agreed and expressly understood by the parties to this treaty—that all the Cherokees and their heirs and descendants to whom any reservations have been made under any former treaties with the United States, and who have not sold or conveyed the same by deed or otherwise and who in the opinion of the commissioners have complied with the terms on which the reservations were granted as far as practicable in the several cases; and which reservations have since been sold by the United States shall constitute a just claim against the United States and the original reservee or their heirs or descendants shall be entitled to receive the present value thereof from the United States as unimproved lands. And all such reservations as have not been sold by the United States and where the terms on which the reservations were made in the opinion of the commissioners have been complied with as far as practicable, they or their heirs or descendants shall be entitled to the same. They are hereby granted and confirmed to them— and also all persons who were entitled to reservations under the treaty of 1817 and who as far as practicable in the opinion of the commissioners, have complied with the stipulations of said treaty, although by the treaty of 1819 such reservations were included in the unceded lands belonging to the Cherokee nation are hereby confirmed to them and they shall be entitled to receive a grant for the same. And all such reservees as were obliged by the laws of the States in which their reservations were situated, to abandon the same or purchase them from the States shall be deemed to have a just claim against the United States for the amount by them paid to the States with interest thereon for such reservations and if obliged to abandon the same, to the present value of such reservations as unimproved lands but in all cases where the reservees have sold their reservations or any part thereof and conveyed the same by deed or otherwise and have been paid for the same, they their heirs or descendants or their assigns shall not be considered as having any claims upon the United States under this article of the treaty nor be entitled to receive any compensation for the lands thus disposed of. It is expressly understood by the parties to this treaty that the amount to be allowed for reservations under this article shall not be deducted out of the consideration money allowed to the Cherokees for their claims for spoliations and the cession of their lands; but the same is to be paid for independently by the United States as it is only a just fulfillment of former treaty stipulations.

ARTICLE 14. It is also agreed on the part of the United States that such warriors of the Cherokee nation as were engaged on the side of the United States in the late war with Great Britain and the southern tribes of Indians, and who were wounded in such service shall be entitled to such pensions as shall be allowed them by the Congress of the United States to commence from the period of their disability.

ARTICLE 15. It is expressly understood and agreed between the parties to this treaty that after deducting the amount which shall be actually expended for the payment for improvements, ferries, claims, for spoliations, removal subsistence and debts and claims upon the Cherokee nation and for the additional quantity of lands and goods for the poorer class of Cherokees and the several sums to be invested for the general national funds; provided for in the several articles of this treaty the balance whatever the same may be shall be equally divided between all the people belonging to the Cherokee nation east according to the census just completed; and such Cherokees as have removed west since June 1833 who are entitled by the terms of their enrollment and removal to all the benefits resulting from the final treaty between the United States and the Cherokees east they shall also be paid for their improvements according to their approved value before their removal where fraud has not already been shown in their valuation.

ARTICLE 16. It is hereby stipulated and agreed by the Cherokees that they shall remove to their new homes within two years from the ratification of this treaty and that during such time the United States shall protect and defend them in their possessions and property and free use and occupation of the same and such persons as have been dispossessed of their improvements and houses; and for which no grant has actually issued previously to the enactment of the law of the State of Georgia, of December 1835 to regulate Indian occupancy shall be again put in possession and placed in the same situation and condition, in reference to the laws of the State of Georgia, as the Indians that have not been dispossessed; and if this is not done, and the people are left unprotected, then the United States shall pay the several Cherokees for their losses and damages sustained by them in consequence thereof. And it is also stipulated and

agreed that the public buildings and improvements on which
they are situated at New Echota for which no grant has been
actually made previous to the passage of the above recited act if
not occupied by the Cherokee people shall be reserved for the
public and free use of the United States and the Cherokee Indians for the purpose of settling and closing all the Indian business arising under this treaty between the commissioners of
claims and the Indians.

The United States, and the several States interested in the
Cherokee lands, shall immediately proceed to survey the lands
ceded by this treaty; but it is expressly agreed and understood
between the parties that the agency buildings and that tract of
land surveyed and laid off for the use of Colonel R. J. Meigs Indian agent or heretofore enjoyed and occupied by his successors
in office shall continue subject to the use and occupancy of the
United States, or such agent as may be engaged specially super-
intending the removal of the tribe.

ARTICLE 17. All the claims arising under or provided for
in the several articles of this treaty, shall be examined and adju-
dicated by such commissioners as shall be appointed by the
President of the United States by and with the advice and consent of the Senate of the United States for that purpose and their
decision shall be final and on their certificate of the amount due
the several claimants they shall be paid by the United States. All
stipulations in former treaties which have not been superseded
or annulled by this shall continue in full force and virtue.

ARTICLE 18. Whereas in consequence of the unsettled
affairs of the Cherokee people and the early frosts, their crops
are insufficient to support their families and great distress is
likely to ensue and whereas the nation will not, until after their
removal be able advantageously to expend the income of the
permanent funds of the nation it is therefore agreed that the
annuities of the nation which may accrue under this treaty for
two years, the time fixed for their removal shall be expended in
provision and clothing for the benefit of the poorer class of the
nation and the United States hereby agree to advance the same
for that purpose as soon after the ratification of this treaty as an
appropriation for the same shall be made. It is however not
intended in this article to interfere with that part of the annuities due the Cherokees west by the treaty of 1819.

ARTICLE 19. This treaty after the same shall be ratified by
the President and Senate of the United States shall be obligatory
on the contracting parties.

ARTICLE 20. [Supplemental article. Stricken out by
Senate.]

In testimony whereof, the commissioners and the chiefs,
head men, and people whose names are hereunto annexed,
being duly authorized by the people in general council

assembled, have affixed their hands and seals for themselves, and in behalf of the Cherokee nation.

I have examined the foregoing treaty, and although not present when it was made, I approve its provisions generally, and therefore sign it.

Wm. Carroll,	Cae-te-hee, his x mark, [L. S.]
J. F. Schermerhorn.	Te-gah-e-ske, his x mark, [L. S.]
Major Ridge, his x mark, [L. S.]	Robert Rogers, [L. S.]
James Foster, his x mark, [L. S.]	John Gunter, [L. S.]
Tesa-ta-esky, his x mark, [L. S.]	John A. Bell, [L. S.]
Charles Moore, his x mark, [L. S.]	Charles F. Foreman, [L. S.]
George Chambers, his x mark, [L. S.]	William Rogers, [L. S.]
Tah-yeske, his x mark, [L. S.]	George W. Adair, [L. S.]
Archilla Smith, his x mark, [L. S.]	Elias Boudinot, [L. S.]
Andrew Ross, [L. S.]	James Starr, his x mark, [L. S.]
William Lassley, [L. S.]	Jesse Half-breed, his x mark. [L. S.]

Signed and sealed in presence of—
Western B. Thomas, secretary.
Ben. F. Currey, special agent.
M. Wolfe Batman, first lieutenant, sixth U. S. infantry,
     disbursing agent.
Jon. L. Hooper, lieutenant, fourth Infantry.
C. M Hitchcock, M.D., assistant surgeon, U.S.A.
G. W. Currey,
Wm. H. Underwood,
Cornelius D. Terhune,
John W. H. Underwood.

Document 7: Letter from Chief John Ross, "To the Senate and House of Representatives," September 28, 1836

The U.S. Senate ratified the Treaty of New Echota, even though the compact was illegitimate, as it was not signed by any duly authorized representative of the Cherokee Nation. When Principal Chief John Ross learned of the treaty, he protested to lawmakers in Washington, and even gathered approximately 15,000 signatures of Cherokee citizens protesting the compact and its ratification, and delivered them to the U.S. capitol. In this letter to the U.S. Congress, Ross explained that the treaty did not represent a binding agreement made by the Cherokee Nation, but rather a document signed by a handful of private individuals, who agreed to a removal settlement that already had been turned down by the elected Cherokee leadership. Calling the treaty "the audacious practices of unprincipled men," Ross explained that enforcing the agreement would be an act of oppression. His letter reflected his faith that the lawmakers, once they realized the true situation, would follow the dictates of justice and compassion and choose not to enforce the treaty. His entreaties, however, were unsuccessful. (Source: *The Papers of Chief John Ross*, vol. 1, ed. Gary E. Moulton [Norman: University of Oklahoma Press, 1985], pp. 458–461.)

> It is well known that for a number of years past we have been harassed by a series of vexations, which it is deemed unnecessary to recite in detail, but the evidence of which our delegation will be prepared to furnish. With a view to bringing our troubles to a close, a delegation was appointed on the 23rd of October, 1835, by the General Council of the nation, clothed with full powers to enter into arrangements with the Government of the United States, for the final adjustment of all our existing difficulties. The delegation failing to effect an arrangement with the United States commissioner, then in the nation, proceeded, agreeably to their instructions in that case, to Washington City, for the purpose of negotiating a treaty with the authorities of the United States.
>
> After the departure of the Delegation, a contract was made by the Rev. John F. Schermerhorn, and certain individual Cherokees, purporting to be a "treaty, concluded at New Echota, in the State of Georgia, on the 29th day of December, 1835, by General William Carroll and John F. Schermerhorn, commissioners on the part of the United States, and the chiefs, headmen, and people of the Cherokee tribes of Indians." A spurious Delegation, in violation of a special injunction of the general council of the nation, proceeded to Washington City with this pretended treaty, and by false and fraudulent representations supplanted in the favor of the Government the legal and accredited Delegation of the Cherokee people, and obtained for this instrument, after making important alterations in its provisions, the recognition of the United States Government. And now it is presented to us as a treaty, ratified by the Senate, and approved by the President, and our acquiescence in its requirements demanded, under the sanction of the displeasure of the United States, and the threat of summary compulsion, in case of refusal. It comes to us, not through our legitimate authorities, the known and usual medium of communication between the Government of the United States and our nation, but through the agency of a complication of powers, civil and military.
>
> By the stipulations of this instrument, we are despoiled of our private possessions, the indefeasible property of individuals.

We are stripped of every attribute of freedom and eligibility for legal self-defence. Our property may be plundered before our eyes; violence may be committed on our persons; even our lives may be taken away, and there is none to regard our complaints. We are denationalized; we are disfranchised. We are deprived of membership in the human family! We have neither land nor home, nor resting place that can be called our own. And this is effected by the provisions of a compact which assumes the venerated, the sacred appellation of treaty.

We are overwhelmed! Our hearts are sickened, our utterance is paralized, when we reflect on the condition in which we are placed, by the audacious practices of unprincipled men, who have managed their stratagems with so much dexterity as to impose on the Government of the United States, in the face of our earnest, solemn, and reiterated protestations.

The instrument in question is not the act of our Nation; we are not parties to its covenants; it has not received the sanction of our people. The makers of it sustain no office nor appointment in our Nation, under the designation of Chiefs, Head men, or any other title, by which they hold, or could acquire, authority to assume the reins of Government, and to make bargain and sale of our rights, our possessions, and our common country. And we are constrained solemnly to declare, that we cannot but contemplate the enforcement of the stipulations of this instrument on us, against our consent, as an act of injustice and oppression, which, we are well persuaded, can never knowingly be countenanced by the Government and people of the United States; nor can we believe it to be the design of these honorable and highminded individuals, who stand at the head of the Govt., to bind a whole Nation, by the acts of a few unauthorized individuals. And, therefore, we, the parties to be affected by the result, appeal with confidence to the justice, the magnanimity, the compassion, of your honorable bodies, against the enforcement, on us, of the provisions of a compact, in the formation of which we have had no agency.

Document 8: Open Letter from Ralph Waldo Emerson, "A Protest Against the Removal of the Cherokee Indians from the State of Georgia," April 23, 1838

Some of the leaders of "Jacksonian" movements vocally denounced the policies that Andrew Jackson put in place and Martin Van Buren followed with regard to the Cherokees. One of these individuals was author, poet, and philosopher Ralph Waldo Emerson.

By 1838, Emerson had established himself as one of the country's leading intellectuals, having created the Transcendental Club, traveled to Europe and met with the likes of William Wordsworth, Thomas Carlyle, and John Stuart Mill, and penned the influential essay "Nature." He was also a leading figure in the city of Concord, Massachusetts; it was from his home there that he wrote to President Van Buren an open letter, published in the press, protesting the removal of the Cherokee Nation. In the letter he asked, "Will the American government steal? Will it lie? Will it kill?" He exhorted the President to abandon plans for coerced removal, which, according to the ratified Treaty of New Echota, could (and did) begin the following month. Throughout the removal debate, Northerners, especially New Englanders, of all U.S. citizens were most likely to oppose removal, in large part because removal was Andrew Jackson's idea. Jackson despised the North, and the feeling was mutual. Emerson, however, was careful to make his arguments against removal nonpartisan and universal. His letter remains one of the most eloquent protests of the removal policy. (Source: The Works of Ralph Waldo Emerson, available at http://www.rwe.org/comm/index.php?option=com_content&task=view&id=79&Itemid=252 [accessed January 12, 2006].)

TO MARTIN VAN BUREN, PRESIDENT OF THE UNITED STATES
Concord, Mass. 23 April, 1838

"Say, what is Honour? 'Tis the finest sense
Of justice which the human mind can frame,
Intent each lurking frailty to disclaim,
And guard the way of life from all offence,
Suffered or done."

SIR: The seat you fill places you in a relation of credit and nearness to every citizen. By right and natural position, every citizen is your friend. Before any acts contrary to his own judgment or interest have repelled the affections of any man, each may look with trust and living anticipation to your government. Each has the highest right to call your attention to such subjects as are of a public nature, and properly belong to the chief magistrate; and the good magistrate will feel a joy in meeting such confidence. In this belief and at the instance of a few of my friends and neighbors, I crave of your patience a short hearing for their sentiments and my own: and the circumstance that my name will be utterly unknown to you will only give the fairer chance to your equitable construction of what I have to say.

Sir, my communication respects the sinister rumors that fill this part of the country concerning the Cherokee people. The interest always felt in the aboriginal population—an interest naturally growing as that decays—has been heightened in regard to this tribe. Even in our distant State some good rumor of their worth and civility has arrived. We have learned with joy their improvement in the social arts. We have read their newspapers. We have seen some of them in our schools and colleges. In common with the great body of the American people, we have witnessed with sympathy the painful labors of these red men to redeem their own race from the doom of eternal inferiority, and to borrow and domesticate in the tribe the arts and customs of the Caucasian race. And notwithstanding the unaccountable apathy with which of late years the Indians have been some-times abandoned to their enemies, it is not to be doubted that it is the good pleasure and the understanding of all humane persons in the Republic, of the men and the matrons sitting in the thriving independent families all over the land, that they shall be duly cared for; that they shall taste justice and love from all to whom we have delegated the office of dealing with them.

The newspapers now inform us that, in December, 1835, a treaty contracting for the exchange of all the Cherokee territory was pre-tended to be made by an agent on the part of the United States with some persons appearing on the part of the Cherokees; that the fact afterwards transpired that these deputies did by no means represent the will of the nation; and that, out of eighteen thousand souls composing the nation, fifteen thousand six hundred and sixty-eight have protested against the so-called treaty. It now appears that the government of the United States choose to hold the Cherokees to this sham treaty, and are proceeding to execute the same. Almost the entire Cherokee Nation stand up and say, "This is not our act. Behold us. Here are we. Do not mistake that handful of deserters for us;" and the American President and the Cabinet, the Senate and the House of Representatives, neither hear these men nor see them, and are contracting to put this active nation into carts and boats, and to drag them over mountains and rivers to a wilderness at a vast distance beyond the Mississippi. And a paper purporting to be an army order fixes a month from this day as the hour for this doleful removal.

In the name of God, sir, we ask you if this be so. Do the newspapers rightly inform us? Men and women with pale and perplexed faces meet one another in the streets and churches here, and ask if this be so. We have inquired if this be a gross misrepresentation from the party opposed to the government and anxious to blacken it with the people. We have looked in the newspapers of different parties and find a horrid confirmation of the tale. We are slow to believe it. We hoped the Indians were misinformed, and that their remonstrance was pre-mature, and will turn out to be a needless act of terror.

The piety, the principle that is left in the United States, if only in its coarsest form, a regard to the speech of men,—forbid us to entertain it as a fact. Such a dereliction of all faith and virtue, such a denial of justice, and such deafness to screams for mercy were never heard of in times of peace and in the dealing of a nation with its own allies and wards, since the earth was made. Sir, does this government think that the people of the United States are become savage and mad? From their mind are the sentiments of love and a good nature wiped clean out? The soul of man, the justice, the mercy that is the heart's heart in all men, from Maine to Georgia, does abhor this business.

In speaking thus the sentiments of my neighbors and my own, perhaps I overstep the bounds of decorum. But would it not be a higher indecorum coldly to argue a matter like this? We only state the fact that a crime is projected that confounds our understandings by its magnitude,—a crime that really deprives us as well as the Cherokees of a country? for how could we call the conspiracy that should crush these poor Indians our government, or the land that was cursed by their parting and dying imprecations our country, any more? You, sir, will bring down that renowned chair in which you sit into infamy if your seal is set to this instrument of perfidy; and the name of this nation, hitherto the sweet omen of religion and liberty, will stink to the world.

You will not do us the injustice of connecting this remonstrance with any sectional and party feeling. It is in our hearts the simplest commandment of brotherly love. We will not have this great and solemn claim upon national and human justice huddled aside under the flimsy plea of its being a party act. Sir, to us the questions upon which the government and the people have been agitated during the past year, touching the prostration of the currency and of trade, seem but motes in comparison. These hard times, it is true, have brought the discussion home to every farmhouse and poor man's house in this town; but it is the chirping of grasshoppers beside the immortal question whether justice shall be done by the race of civilized to the race of savage man,—whether all the attributes of reason, of civility, of justice, and even of mercy, shall be put off by the American people, and so vast an outrage upon the Cherokee Nation and upon human nature shall be consummated.

One circumstance lessens the reluctance with which I intrude at this time on your attention my conviction that the government ought to be admonished of a new historical fact, which the discussion of this question has disclosed, namely, that there exists in a great part of the Northern people a gloomy diffidence in the moral character of the government.

On the broaching of this question, a general expression of despondency, of disbelief that any good will accrue from a remonstrance on an act of fraud and robbery, appeared in those men to whom we naturally turn for aid and counsel. Will the American government steal? Will it lie? Will it kill?—We ask triumphantly. Our counsellors and old statesmen here say that ten years ago they would have staked their lives on the affirmation that the proposed Indian measures could not be executed; that the unanimous country would put them down. And now the steps of this crime follow each other so fast, at such fatally quick time, that the millions of virtuous citizens, whose agents the government are, have no place to interpose, and must shut their eyes until the last howl and wailing of these tormented villages and tribes shall afflict the ear of the world.

I will not hide from you, as an indication of the alarming distrust, that a letter addressed as mine is, and suggesting to the mind of the Executive the plain obligations of man, has a burlesque character in the apprehensions of some of my friends. I, sir, will not beforehand treat you with the contumely of this distrust. I will at least state to you this fact, and show you how plain and humane people, whose love would be honor, regard the policy of the government, and what injurious inferences they draw as to the minds of the governors. A man with your experience in affairs must have seen cause to appreciate the futility of opposition to the moral sentiment. However feeble the sufferer and however great the oppressor, it is in the nature of things that the blow should recoil upon the aggressor. For God is in the sentiment, and it cannot be withstood. The potentate and the people perish before it; but with it, and as its executor, they are omnipotent.

I write thus, sir, to inform you of the state of mind these Indian tidings have awakened here, and to pray with one voice more that you, whose hands are strong with the delegated power of fifteen millions of men, will avert with that might the terrific injury which threatens the Cherokee tribe.

With great respect, sir, I am your fellow citizen,
RALPH WALDO EMERSON

Document 9: General Winfield Scott's Address to the Cherokee Nation, May 10, 1838

U.S. General Winfield Scott was ordered to oversee the removal process. It was, as he said, a "painful duty" for him, and he immediately appreciated the potential for violence and bloodshed inherent in the endeavor. He was particularly wary of the troops from Georgia, and feared they were especially likely to abuse their positions of power over the Cherokees. He ordered his men to be professional in carrying out their orders. He also issued a general statement to all

Cherokees nearly two weeks before the removal process began. His address seemed to be both warning and plea: a warning of how dangerous the situation was, and a plea to cooperate and not exacerbate the already tense situation. Although he encouraged families to relocate voluntarily to removal sites, there was little time: the military roundups followed less than two weeks after his address. It seems likely that his address was meant as much for his troops as for the Cherokees, in particular his poignant request that he not be forced to witness "the destruction of the Cherokees." Although violence certainly played a part in the loss of life related to removal, the terrible conditions in the containment camps and on the route West contributed significantly to the fatal forces of disease, exposure, and starvation. Scott soon turned over control of the process to the Cherokees. (Source: Available at http://www.cviog.uga.edu/Projects/gainfo/scottadd. htm [accessed February 2, 2006]. Also cited in *A Wilderness Still the Cradle of Nature: Frontier Georgia*, ed. Edward J. Cashin [Savannah, GA: Beehive Press, 1994], pp. 137–138.)

Cherokees! The President of the United States has sent me with a powerful army, to cause you, in obedience to the treaty of 1835, to join that part of your people who have already established in prosperity on the other side of the Mississippi. Unhappily, the two years which were allowed for the purpose, you have suffered to pass away without following, and without making any preparation to follow; and now, or by the time that this solemn address shall reach your distant settlements, the emigration must be commenced in haste, but I hope without disorder. I have no power, by granting a farther delay, to correct the error that you have committed. The full moon of May is already on the wane; and before another shall have passed away, every Cherokee man, woman and child in those states must be in motion to join their brethren in the far West.

My friends! This is no sudden determination on the part of the President, whom you and I must now obey. By the treaty, the emigration was to have been completed on or before the 23rd of this month; and the President has constantly kept you warned, during the two years allowed, through all his officers and agents in this country, that the treaty would be enforced.

I am come to carry out that determination. My troops already occupy many positions in the country that you are to abandon, and thousands and thousands are approaching from every quarter, to render resistance and escape alike hopeless. All those troops, regular and militia, are your friends. Receive them and confide in them as such. Obey them when they tell you that you can remain no longer in this country. Soldiers are as kindhearted as brave, and the desire of every one of us is to execute our painful duty in mercy. We are commanded by the President to act towards you in that spirit, and much is also the wish of the whole people of America.

Chiefs, head-men and warriors! Will you then, by resistance, compel us to resort to arms? God forbid! Or will you, by flight, seek to hid yourselves in mountains and forests, and thus oblige us to hunt you down? Remember that, in pursuit, it may be impossible to avoid conflicts. The blood of the white man or the blood of the red man may be spilt, and, if spilt, however accidentally, it may be impossible for the discreet and humane among you, or among us, to prevent a general war and carnage. Think of this, my Cherokee brethren! I am an old warrior, and have been present at many a scene of slaughter, but spare me, I beseech you, the horror of witnessing the destruction of the Cherokees.

Do not, I invite you, even wait for the close approach of the troops; but make such preparations for emigration as you can and hasten to this place, to Ross's Landing or to Gunter's Landing, where you all will be received in kindness by officers selected for the purpose. You will find food for all and clothing for the destitute at either of those places, and thence at your ease and in comfort be transported to your new homes, according to the terms of the treaty.

This is the address of a warrior to warriors. May his entreaties be kindly received and may the God of both prosper the Americans and Cherokees and preserve them long in peace and friendship with each other!

Document 10: The Constitution of the Cherokee Nation, September 6, 1839

Upon reaching Indian Territory, the Cherokees adopted a new constitution. This document both replaced the 1827 constitution for the Cherokees who had survived the Trail of Tears, and served as a new compact for the "Old Settlers," those Cherokees who had moved west previously. Thus both sets of Cherokees were united under this compact in Indian Territory. The constitution was altered after the U.S. Civil War to reflect the abolishment of slavery, but continued to be the nation's compact until a new constitution was ratified by the Cherokee Nation of Oklahoma in 1975. It is one of the great ironies of the Trail of Tears story that the Cherokees would choose to pattern their post-removal constitution so closely after the U.S. Constitution, considering the fact that they had in effect witnessed two examples of the failure of the U.S. political system, first when the

Worcester v. Georgia decision was not enforced, and second when the U.S. Senate ratified the illegitimate Treaty of New Echota. (Source: Available at http://www.cherokeeobserver.org/Issues/1839 constitution.html [accessed October 12, 2005].)

The Eastern and Western Cherokees having again re-united, and become one body politic, under the style and title of the Cherokee Nation: Therefore,

We, the people of the Cherokee Nation, in National Convention assembled, in order to establish justice, insure tranquility, promote the common welfare, and secure to ourselves and our posterity the blessings of freedom acknowledging, with humility and gratitude, the goodness of the Sovereign Ruler of the Universe in permitting us so to do, and imploring His aid and guidance in its accomplishment—do ordain and establish this Constitution for the government of the Cherokee Nation.

ARTICLE I.

Sec. 1. The boundary of the Cherokee Nation shall be that described in the treaty of 1833 between the United States and Western Cherokees, subject to such extension as may be made in the adjustment of the unfinished business with the United States.

Sec. 2. The lands of the Cherokee Nation shall remain common property; but the improvements made thereon, and in the possession of the citizens respectively who made, or may rightfully be in possession of them: Provided, that the citizens of the Nation possessing exclusive and indefeasible right to their improvements, as expressed in this article, shall possess no right or power to dispose of their improvements, in any manner whatever, to the United States, individual States, or to individual citizens thereof; and that, whenever any citizen shall remove with his effects out of the limits of this Nation, and become a citizen of any other government, all his rights and privileges as a citizen of this Nation shall cease: Provided, nevertheless, That the National Council shall have power to re-admit, by law, to all the rights of citizenship, any such person or persons who may, at any time, desire to return to the Nation, on memorializing the National Council for such readmission.

ARTICLE II.

Sec. 1. The power of the Government shall be divided into three distinct departments—the Legislative, the Executive, and the Judicial.

Sec. 2. No person or persons belonging to one of these departments shall exercise any of the powers properly belonging to either of the others, except in the cases hereinafter expressly directed or permitted.

ARTICLE III.

Sec. 1. The Legislative power shall be vested in two distinct branches—a National Committee, and Council; and the style of their acts shall be—Be it enacted by the National Council.

Sec. 2. The National Council shall make provisions, by law, for laying off the Cherokee Nation into eight districts; and if subsequently it should be deemed expedient, one or two may be added thereto.

Sec. 3. The National Committee shall consist of two members from each district, and the Council shall consist of three members from each District, to be chosen by the qualified electors in their respective Districts for two years; the elections to be held in the respective Districts every two years, at such times and place as may be directed by law.

The National Council shall, after the present year, be held annually, to be convened on the first Monday in October, at such place as may be designated by the National Council, or, in case of emergency, the Principal Chief.

Sec. 4. Before the Districts shall be laid off, any election which may take place shall be by a general vote of the electors throughout the Nation for all offices to be elected.

The first election for all three officers of the Government— Chiefs, Executive Council, members of the National Council, Judges and Sheriffs—shall be held at Tah-le-quah before the rising of this Convention; and the term of service of all officers elected previous to the first Monday in October 1839, shall be extended to embrace, in addition to the regular constitutional term, the time intervening from their election to the first Monday in October, 1839.

Sec. 5. No person shall be eligible to a seat in the National Council but a free Cherokee Male citizen who shall have attained the age of twenty-five years.

The descendants of Cherokee men by free women except the African race, whose parents may have been living together as man and wife, according to the customs and laws of this Nation, shall be entitled to all the rights and privileges of this Nation, as well as the posterity of Cherokee women by all free men. No person who is negro and mulatto parentage, either by the father or mother's side, shall be eligible to hold any office of profit, honor or trust under this Government.

Sec. 6. The electors and members of the National Council shall in all cases, except those of treason, felony, or breach of the peace, be privileged from arrest during their attendance at elections, and at the National Council, in going to and returning.

Sec. 7. In all elections by the people, the electors shall vote viva voce.

All free males citizens [sic], who shall have attained to the age of eighteen [18] years shall be equally entitled to vote at all public elections.

Sec. 8. Each branch of the National Council, when assembled, shall judge of the qualifications and returns of its own members; and determine the rules of its proceedings; punish a member for disorderly behavior, and with the concurrence of two thirds, expel a member; but not a second time for the same offense.

Sec. 9. Each branch of the National Council, when assembled, shall choose its own officers; a majority of each shall constitute a quorum to do business, but a smaller number may adjourn from day to day and compel the attendance of absent members in such manner and under such penalty as each branch may prescribe.

Sec. 10. The members of the National Council, shall each receive from the public Treasury a compensation for their services which shall be three dollars per day during their attendance at the National Council; and the members of the Council shall each receive three dollars per day for their services during their attendance at the National Council, provided that the same may be increased or diminished by law, but no alteration shall take effect during the period of service of the members of the National Council by whom such alteration may have been made.

Sec. 11. The National Council shall regulate by law by whom and in what manner, writs of elections shall be issued to fill the vacancies which may happen in either branch thereof.

Sec. 12. Each member of the National Council, before he takes his seat, shall take the following oath, or affirmation: I, A.B. do solemnly swear (or affirm, as the case may be,) that I have not obtained my election by bribing, treats, or any undue and unlawful means used by myself or others by my desire or approbation for that purpose; that I consider myself constitutionally qualified as a member of ____, and that on all questions and measures which may come before me I will so give my vote and so conduct myself as in my judgment shall appear most conducive to the interest and prosperity of this Nation, and I will bear true faith and allegiance to the same, and to the utmost of my ability and power observe, conform to, support and defend the Constitution thereof.

Sec. 13. No person who may be convicted of felony shall be eligible to any office or appointment of honor, profit, or trust within this Nation.

Sec. 14. The National Council shall have the power to make laws and regulations which they shall deemed necessary and proper for the good of the Nation, which shall not be contrary to this Constitution.

Sec. 15. It shall be the duty of the National Council to pass laws as may be necessary and proper to decide differences by arbitration, to be appointed by the parties, who may choose that summary mode of adjustment.

Sec. 16. No power of suspending the laws of this Nation shall be exercised, unless by the National Council or its authority.

Sec. 17. No retrospective law, nor any law impairing the obligation of contracts, shall be passed.

Sec. 18. The National Council shall have the power to make laws for laying and collecting taxes, for the purpose of raising a revenue.

Sec. 19. All bills making appropriations shall originate in the National Committee, but the Council may propose amendments or reject the same; all other bills may originate in either branch, subject to the concurrence or rejection of the other.

Sec. 20. All acknowledged treaties shall be the supreme laws of the land, and the National Council shall have the sole power of deciding on the construction of all treaty stipulations.

Sec. 21. The Council shall have the sole power of impeachment. All impeachments shall be tried by the National Committee. When setting for that purpose the member shall be upon oath or affirmation; and no person shall be convicted without the concurrence of two-thirds of the members present.

Sec. 22. The Principal Chief, assistant Principal Chief, and all civil officers shall be liable to impeachment for misdemeanor in office; but judgment in such cases shall not be extended further than removal from office and disqualification to hold office of honor, trust, or profit under the Government of this Nation.

The party, whether convicted or acquitted, shall nevertheless, be liable to indictment, trial, judgment and punishment according to law.

ARTICLE IV.

Sec. 1. The Supreme Executive Power of this Nation shall be vested in a Principal Chief, who shall be styled the Principal Chief of the Cherokee Nation.

The Principal Chief shall hold office for the term of four years; and shall be elected by the qualified electors on the same day and at the places where they shall respectively vote for members of the National Council.

The returns of the election for Principal Chief shall be sealed up and directed to the President of the National Committee, who shall open and publish them in the presence of the National Council assembled. The person having the highest number of votes shall be Principal Chief; but if two or more shall be equal and highest in votes, one of them shall be chosen by joint vote of both branches of the Council. The manner of determining contested elections shall be directed by law.

Sec. 2. No person except a natural born citizen shall be eligible to the office of Principal Chief; neither shall any person be eligible to that office who shall not have attained the age of thirty-five years.

Sec. 3. There shall also be chosen at the same time by the qualified electors in the same manner for four years, an assistant Principal Chief, who shall have attained to the age of thirty-five years.

Sec. 4. In case of the removal of the Principal Chief from office, or of his death or resignation, or inability to discharge the powers and duties of the said office, the same shall devolve on the assistant Principal Chief until the disability be removed or a Principal Chief shall be elected.

Sec. 5. The National Council may by law provide for the case of removal, death, resignation, or disability of both the Principal Chief and assistant Principal Chief, declaring what officer shall then act as Principal Chief until the disability be removed or a Principal Chief shall be elected.

Sec. 6. The Principal Chief and assistant Principal Chief shall, at stated times, receive for their services a compensation which shall neither be increased nor diminished during the period for which they shall have been elected; and they shall not receive within that period any other emolument from the Cherokee Nation or any other Government.

Sec. 7. Before the Principal Chief enters on the execution of his office, he shall take the following oath or affirmation:

"I do solemnly swear, or affirm, that I will faithfully execute the duties of Principal Chief of the Cherokee Nation, and will, to the best of my ability, preserve, protect, and defend the Constitution of the Cherokee Nation."

Sec. 8. He may, on extraordinary occasions, convene the National Council at the seat of government.

Sec. 9. He shall from time to time, give to the National Council information of the state of government, and recommend to their consideration such measures as he may deem expedient.

Sec. 10. He shall take care that the laws be faithfully executed.

Sec. 11. It shall be his duty to visit the different districts at least once in two years, to inform himself of the general condition of the country.

Sec. 12. The assistant Principal Chief shall, by virtue of his office, aid and advise the Principal Chief in the administration of the government at all times during his continuance in office.

Sec. 13. Vacancies that may occur in offices, the appointment of which is vested in the National Council, shall be filled by the Principal Chief during the recess of the National Council by granting commissions which shall expire at the end of the next session thereof.

Sec. 14. Every bill which shall pass both branches of the National Council shall, before it becomes a law, be presented to the Principal Chief; if he approves, he shall sign it; but if not, he shall return it, with his objections to that branch in which it may have originated, who shall enter the objections at large on their journals and proceed to reconsider it; if, after such reconsideration, two-thirds of that branch shall agree to pass the bill, it shall be sent, together with the objections, to the other branch, by which it shall likewise be reconsidered, and, if approved by two-thirds of that branch, it shall become law. If any bill shall not be returned by the Principal Chief within five days (Sundays excepted), after the same has been presented to him, it shall become a law in like manner as if he had signed it, unless the National Council, by their adjournment, prevent its return, in which case it shall be a law, unless sent back within three days after their next meeting.

Sec. 15. Members of the National Council, and all officers, executive and judicial, shall be bound by oath to support the Constitution of this Nation, and to perform the duties of their respective offices with fidelity.

Sec. 16. In case of disagreement between the two branches of the National Council with respect to the time of adjournment, the Principal Chief shall have power to adjourn the same to such time as he may deem proper; provided, it be not a period beyond the next constitutional meeting thereof.

Sec. 17. The Principal Chief shall, during the session of the National Council, attend at the seat of government.

Sec. 18. There shall be a council composed of five persons, to be appointed by the National Council, whom the Principal Chief shall have full power at his discretion to assemble; he, together with the Assistant Principal Chief and the counselors, or a majority of them, may, from time to time, hold and keep a council for ordering and directing the affairs of the Nation according to law; provided, the National Council shall have power to reduce the number, if deemed expedient, after the first term of service, to a number not less than three.

Sec. 19. The members or the executive council shall be chosen for the term of two years.

Sec. 20. The resolutions and advice of the council shall be recorded in a register, and signed by the members agreeing thereto, which may be called for by either branch of the National Council; and any counselor may enter his dissent to the majority.

Sec. 21. The Treasurer shall, before, entering on the duties of his office, give bond to the Nation, with sureties, to the satisfaction of the National Council, for the faithful discharge of his trust.

Sec. 22. The Treasurer shall, before entering on the duties of his office, give bond to the Nation, with sureties, to the satisfaction of the National Council, for the faithful discharge of his trust.

Sec. 23. No money shall be drawn from the Treasury but by warrant from the Principal Chief, and in consequence of appropriations made by law.

Sec. 24. It shall be the duty of the Treasurer to receive all public moneys, and to make a regular statement and account of the receipts and expenditures of all public moneys at the annual session of the National Council.

ARTICLE V.

Sec. 1. The Judicial Powers shall be vested in a Supreme Court, and such circuit and inferior courts as the National Council may, from time to time, ordain and establish.

Sec. 2. The judges of the Supreme and Circuit courts shall hold their commissions for the term of four years, but any of them may be removed from office on the address of two-thirds of each branch of the National Council to the Principal Chief for that purpose.

Sec. 3. The Judges of the Supreme and Circuit Courts shall, at stated times, receive a compensation which shall not be diminished during their continuance in office, but they shall receive no fees or perquisites of office, nor hold any other office of profit or trust under the government of this Nation, or any other power.

Sec. 4. No person shall be appointed a judge of any of the courts until he shall have attained the age of thirty years.

Sec. 5. The Judges of the Supreme and Circuit courts shall be as many Justices of the Peace as it may be deemed expedient for the public good, whose powers, duties, and duration in office shall be clearly designated by law.

Sec. 6. The Judges of the Supreme Court and of the Circuit Courts shall have complete criminal jurisdiction in such cases, and in such manner as may be pointed out by law.

Sec. 7. No Judge shall sit on trial of any cause when the parties are connected [with him] by affinity or consanguinity, except by consent of the parties. In case all the Judges of the Supreme Courts shall be interested in the issue of any case, or related to all or either of the parties, the National Council may provide by law for the selection of a suitable number of persons of good character and knowledge, for the determination thereof, and who shall be specially commissioned for the adjudication of such cases by the Principal Chief.

Sec. 8. All writs and other process shall run "In the Name of the Cherokee Nation," and bear test and be signed by the respective clerks.

Sec. 9. Indictments shall conclude—"Against the Peace and Dignity of the Cherokee Nation."

Sec. 10. The Supreme Court shall, after the present year, hold its session annually at the seat of government, to convened on the first Monday of October in each year.

Sec. 11. In all criminal prosecutions the accused shall have the right of being heard; of demanding the nature and cause of the accusation; of meeting the witnesses face to face; of having compulsory process for obtaining witnesses in his or their favor; and in prosecutions by indictment or information, a speedy public trial, by an impartial jury of the vicinage; nor shall the accused be compelled to give evidence against himself.

Sec. 12. The people shall be secure in their persons, houses, papers, and possessions from unreasonable seizures and searches, and no warrant to search any place, or to seize any person or thing, shall issue, without describing them as nearly as may be, nor without good cause, supported by oath or affirmation.

Sec. 13. All persons shall be bilabial by sufficient securities, unless for capital offenses, where the proof is evident or presumption great.

ARTICLE VI.

Sec. 1. No person who denies the being of a God or future state of reward and punishment, shall hold any office in the civil department in this Nation.

Sec. 2. The free exercise of religious worship, and serving God without distinction, shall forever be enjoyed within the limits of this Nation; provided, that this liberty of conscience shall not be so construed as to excuse acts of licentiousness, or justify practices inconsistent with the peace or safety of this Nation.

Sec. 3. When the National Council shall determine the expediency of appointing delegates, or other public agents, for the purpose of transacting business with the government of the United States, the Principal Chief shall appoint and commission such delegates or public agents accordingly. On all matters of interest, touching the rights of the citizens of this Nation, which may require the attention of the United States government, the Principal Chief shall keep up a friendly correspondence with that government through the medium of its proper officers.

Sec. 4. All commissions shall be "In the name and by the Authority of the Cherokee Nation," and be sealed with the seal of the Nation, and signed by the Principal Chief. The Principal Chief shall make use of his private seal until a National seal shall be provided.

Sec. 5. A sheriff shall be elected in each district by the qualified electors thereof, who shall hold his office two years, unless sooner removed. Should a vacancy occur subsequent to an election, it shall be filled by the Principal Chief, as in other cases, and the person so appointed shall continue in office until the next regular election.

Sec. 6. No person shall, for the same offense, be twice put in jeopardy of life or limb; nor shall the property of any person be taken and applied to public use without a just and fair compensation; provided, that nothing in this clause shall be construed as to impair the right and power of the National Council to lay and collect taxes.

Sec. 7. The right of trial by jury shall remain inviolate, and every person, for injury sustained in person, property, or reputation, shall have remedy by due process of law.

Sec. 8. The appointment of all officers, not otherwise directed by this Constitution, shall be vested in the National Council.

Sec. 9. Religion, mortality and knowledge being necessary to good government, the preservation of liberty, and the happiness of mankind, schools and the means of education shall forever be encouraged in this Nation.

Sec. 10. The National Council may propose such amendments to this Constitution as two-thirds of each branch may deem expedient, and the Principal Chief shall issue a proclamation, directing all civil officers of the several districts to promulgate the same as extensively as possible within their respective districts at least six months previous to the next general election. And if, at the first session of the National Council, after such general election, two-thirds of each branch shall, by ayes and noes, ratify such proposed amendments, they shall be valid to all intent and purposes, as parts of this Constitution; provided that such proposed amendments shall be read on three several days in each branch, as well when the same are proposed, as when they are ratified.

Done in convention at Tahlequah, Cherokee Nation, this sixth day of September, 1839,

GEORGE LOWREY
President of the National Convention

Document 11: Letter from William Shorey Coodey (Cherokee), August 13, 1840

Personal accounts from the Trail of Tears reflect the horror of the event. This letter was written by William Shorey Coodey, a nephew of Principal Chief John Ross. Coodey previously had represented the Cherokee Nation in Washington, where he traveled to protest the state of Georgia's encroachment into Cherokee lands. He wrote the letter to a non-Cherokee family friend, John Howard Payne, who not only was sympathetic to the Cherokees' plight, but had suffered firsthand when he had been arrested along with John Ross in 1835 by the Georgia guard, illegally detained, harassed, and then eventually freed. Although Coodey's account lacks the graphic details of other eyewitness narratives, it captures well the despair and hopelessness of those who embarked on the Trail of Tears, and places clear blame for the experience on the "cravings of avarice." Coodey was involved with the creation of the Cherokee

Constitutions of 1827 and 1839. He died in 1849, while serving as the Cherokee delegate to the U.S. Congress; his pallbearers included supporters John C. Calhoun, Henry Clay, and Daniel Webster. (Source: From a letter to John Howard Payne, Payne/Butrick Mss., vol. 6, Ayer collection, Newberry Library, Chicago; cited in *Voices from the Trail of Tears*, ed. Vicki Rozema [Winston-Salem, NC: John F. Blair, 2003], pp. 133–135.)

The entire Cherokee population were captured by the U.S. troops under General Scott in 1838 and marched, to principally, upon the border of Tennessee where they were encamped in large bodies until the time for their final removal west. At one of these encampments, twelve miles south of the Agency, and Head Quarters of Genl. Scott, was organised the first detachment for marching under the arrangement committing the whole management of the emigration into the hands of the Cherokees themselves.

The first of Septer. was fixed as the time for a part to be in motion on the route. Much anxiety was felt, and great exertions made by the Cherokees to comply with everything reasonably to be expected of them, and it was determined that the first detachment should move in the last days of August. . . .

At noon all was in readiness for moving. The trains were stretched out in a line along the road through a heavy forest, groups of persons formed about each waggon, others shaking the hand of some sick friend or relative who would be left behind. The temporary camps covered with boards and some of bark, that for three summer months had been their only shelter and *home* were crackling and falling under a blazing flame. The day was bright and beautiful, but a gloomy thoughtfulness was strongly depicted in the lineaments of every face. In all the bustle of preparation there was a silence and stillness of the voice that betrayed the sadness of the heart.

At length the word was given to *move on*. I glanced along the line and the form of Going Snake, an aged and respected chief whose head eighty winters had whitened, mounted on his favorite poney passed before me and lead the way in advance, followed by a number of young men on horse back.

At this very moment a low sound of distant thunder fell on my ear. In almost an exact western direction a dark spiral cloud was rising above the horizon and sent forth a murmur. I almost fancied a voice of Divine indignation for the wrongs of my poor and unhappy countrymen, driven by brutal power from all they loved and cherished in the land of their fathers, to gratify the cravings of avarice. The sun was unclouded—no rain fell—the thunder rolled away and sounds hushed in the distance.

SELECTED BIBLIOGRAPHY

Primary Sources

Boudinot, Elias. *Cherokee Editor: The Writings of Elias Boudinot*. Ed. Theda Perdue. Knoxville: University of Tennessee Press, 1983. Collects most of Elias Boudinot's published writings, including letters, articles, editorials, and pamphlets.

Dale, Edward Everett, and Gaston Litton, eds. *Cherokee Cavaliers: Forty Years of Cherokee History as Told in the Correspondence of the Ridge-Watie-Boudinot Family*. Norman: University of Oklahoma Press, 1939. Reprints the personal correspondence of key figures in the Treaty Party.

Jackson, Andrew. *The Papers of Andrew Jackson*. Ed. Sam B. Smith, Harriet Fason Chappell Owsley, and Harold D. Moser. 6 vols. Knoxville: University of Tennessee Press, 1980–. Offers the authoritative collection of Andrew Jackson's papers.

Jefferson, Thomas. *The Complete Jefferson*. Ed. Saul K. Padover. New York: Duell, Sloan, and Pearce, 1943. Includes Thomas Jefferson's major writings, published and unpublished, with the exception of his letters.

Perdue, Theda, and Michael D. Green, eds. *The Cherokee Removal: A Brief History with Documents*. 2nd ed. New York: Bedford/St. Martin's, 2005. Provides the best single-volume collection of documents regarding the Trail of Tears, from both U.S. and Cherokee perspectives.

Ross, John. *The Papers of Chief John Ross*, vols. 1 and 2. Ed. Gary E. Moulton. Norman: University of Oklahoma Press, 1985.

Rozema, Vicki. *Voices from the Trail of Tears*. Winston-Salem, NC: John F. Blair, 2003. Offers an overview of the Trail of Tears through primary documents, focused primarily on the experience of removal.

Worcester, Samuel A. *New Echota Letters: Contributions of Samuel A. Worcester to the Cherokee Phoenix*. Ed. Jack Frederick Kilpatrick and Anna

Gritts Kilpatrick. Dallas: Southern Methodist University Press, 1968. Compiles the writings of missionary Samuel A. Worcester as published in *The Cherokee Phoenix.*

Trail of Tears Studies

Anderson, William L., ed. *Cherokee Removal: Before and After.* Athens: University of Georgia Press, 1991. Offers a series of essays by scholars on different aspects of the Trail of Tears, from demographics to rhetoric.

Burke, Joseph C. "The Cherokee Cases: A Study in Law, Politics, and Morality." *Stanford Law Review* 21 (1969): 500–531. Examines *Cherokee Nation v. Georgia* and *Worcester v. Georgia.*

Debo, Angie. *And Still the Waters Run: The Betrayal of the Five Civilized Tribes.* Princeton, NJ: Princeton University Press, 1940. Provides the classic account of the dispossession of the Cherokee, Choctaw, Creek, Chickasaw, and Seminole nations.

Ehle, John. *The Trail of Tears: The Rise and Fall of the Cherokee Nation.* New York: Doubleday, 1988. Gives a one-volume account of the story of Cherokee removal.

Foreman, Grant. *Indian Removal.* Norman: University of Oklahoma Press, 1932. Offers the standard one-volume examination of the Cherokee, Choctaw, Creek, Chickasaw, and Seminole removals.

Horsman, Reginald. *The Origin of Indian Removal, 1815–1824.* East Lansing: Michigan State University Press, 1970. Based on a lecture, examines earlier events that made the Trail of Tears possible.

Howard, R. Palmer, and Virginia E. Allen. "Stress and Death in the Settlement of Indian Territory." *Chronicles of Oklahoma* 53 (1975): 492–515. Considers from a medical perspective the physical and psychological challenges of those removed.

Hutchins, John. "The Trial of Samuel Austin Worcester." *Journal of Cherokee Studies* 2 (1977): 356–374. Investigates in depth Samuel Worcester's legal role in the story of removal.

Jahoda, Gloria. *The Trail of Tears: The Story of the American Indian Removals, 1813–1855.* New York: Wings Books, 1975. Gives a one-volume account of removal, including the Cherokee Trail of Tears, and offers a selection of relevant government documents in the appendix.

Knight, Oliver. "Cherokee Society under the Stress of Removal, 1820–1846." *Chronicles of Oklahoma* 32 (1954–1955): 414–428. Considers the effects of the Trail of Tears on the internal workings of Cherokee society.

McLoughlin, William G. *After the Trail of Tears: The Cherokees' Struggle for Sovereignty, 1839–1880.* Chapel Hill: University of North Carolina

Press, 1993. Explores the political challenges faced by the Cherokee Nation after the Trail of Tears.

————. *Cherokee Renascence in the New Republic.* Princeton, NJ: Princeton University Press, 1986. Investigates the reinvention of the Cherokee Nation, including the creation of the constitution and the literacy revolution.

————. *Cherokees and Christianity, 1794–1870: Essays on Acculturation and Cultural Persistence.* Athens: University of Georgia Press, 1994. Examines the influence of Christianity on the Cherokee Nation before, during, and after removal.

Memmi, Albert. *The Colonizer and the Colonized.* Trans. Howard Greenfeld. New York: Orion, 1965. Theorizes about the power relationship between colonizers and those who are colonized.

Monteith, Carmeleta L. "Literacy among the Cherokee in the Early Nineteenth Century." *Journal of Cherokee Studies* 9, no. 2 (Fall 1984): 56–75. Studies the nature of the Cherokee literacy revolution.

Mooney, James. *Historical Sketch of the Cherokee.* Chicago: Aldine, 1975. Provides research from the leading early ethnologist of the Cherokees, including accounts by survivors as related to James Mooney.

————. "Myths of the Cherokees." In Smithsonian Institution, Bureau of American Ethnology. *Nineteenth Annual Report, 1897–1898.* Part I, pp. 3–576. Washington, D.C.: U.S. Government Printing Office, 1900. Gives accounts of stories told by Cherokees to ethnologist James Mooney, from myths to historical tales.

Norgren, Jill. *The Cherokee Cases: The Confrontation of Law and Politics.* New York: McGraw-Hill, 1996. Provides a legal history of *Cherokee Nation v. Georgia* and *Worcester v. Georgia.*

Perdue, Theda. "The Conflict Within: The Cherokee Power Structure and Removal." *Georgia Historical Quarterly* 73 (Fall 1989): 465–491. Considers the internal factions within the Cherokee Nation exacerbated by removal.

Prucha, Francis Paul. "Andrew Jackson's Indian Policy: A Reassessment." *Journal of American History* 56 (1969): 527–539. Focuses on Andrew Jackson's commitment to removal.

Rogin, Michael Paul. *Fathers and Children: Andrew Jackson and the Subjugation of the American Indian.* New York: Knopf, 1975. Examines the paternalism of Andrew Jackson's policy toward Native America.

Satz, Ronald N. *American Indian Policy in the Jacksonian Era.* Lincoln: University of Nebraska Press, 1975. Considers Andrew Jackson's policy from both an ethnohistorical and a public administration perspective.

Wallace, Anthony F. C. *The Long Bitter Trail: Andrew Jackson and the Indians.* New York: Hill and Wang, 1993. Explores Andrew Jackson's position on "the Indian question" and how it influenced his policies.

Young, Mary. "Indian Removal and the Attack on Tribal Autonomy: The Cherokee Case." In *Indians of the Lower South: Past and Present*, ed. John K. Mahon, pp. 125–142. Pensacola, FL: Gulf Coast History and Humanities Conference, 1975. Examines the ways in which removal affected Cherokee autonomy.

Biographies of Key Figures

Anderson, Mabel W. *The Life of General Stand Watie and Contemporary Cherokee History*. Pryor, OK: Mayes County Republican, 1931. Offers a biography of Elias Boudinot's brother and Treaty Party member, Stand Watie.

Bird, Traveller. *Tell Them They Lie: The Sequoyah Myth*. Los Angeles: Westernlore, 1971. Offers an unusual perspective on Sequoyah and his syllabary, proving how Sequoyah remains a powerful and contested figure in Cherokee history.

Burstein, Andrew. *The Passions of Andrew Jackson*. New York: Knopf, 2003. Examines Andrew Jackson and his personal life from a psychological perspective, and considers how his personality affected his performance as a political leader.

Eaton, Rachel Caroline. *John Ross and the Cherokee Indians*. Menasha, WI: George Banta, 1914. Explores the legacy of Cherokee Principal Chief John Ross.

Fogelson, Raymond D. "On the Varieties of Indian History: Sequoyah and Traveller Bird." *Journal of Ethnic Studies* 2 (1974): 105–112. Considers the history provided in the book *Tell Them They Lie: The Sequoyah Myth*.

Foreman, Grant. *Sequoyah*. Norman: University of Oklahoma Press, 1938. Offers the traditional account of Sequoyah's life.

Foster, George Everett. *Se-Quo-Yah, the American Cadmus and Modern Moses: A Complete Biography of the Greatest of Redmen, around Whose Wonderful Life Has Been Woven the Manners, Customs, and Beliefs of the Early Cherokees Together with a Recital of Their Wrongs and Wonderful Progress toward Civilization*. Philadelphia: Indian Rights Association, 1885. Gives an early account of Sequoyah and the Cherokee literacy revolution.

Franks, Kenny A. *Stand Watie and the Agony of the Cherokee Nation*. Memphis: Memphis State University Press, 1979. Considers the brother of Elias Boudinot and Treaty Party member, Stand Watie, especially in the aftermath of the Trail of Tears.

Gabriel, Ralph Henry. *Elias Boudinot: Cherokee and His America*. Norman: University of Oklahoma Press, 1941. Provides the standard account of the life of Elias Boudinot.

Kilpatrick, Jack Frederick. *Sequoyah of Earth And Intellect.* Austin: Encino Press, 1965. Gives another variation on the story of Sequoyah and his importance to the Cherokee Nation.

Luebke, Barbara F. "Elias Boudinot and 'Indian Removal'." In *Outsiders in Nineteenth-Century Press History: Multicultural Perspectives.* Bowling Green, OH: Bowling Green State University Popular Press, 1995: 115–144. Examines Elias Boudinot's position on and actions about the removal issue.

Moulton, Gary E. *John Ross: Cherokee Chief.* Athens: University of Georgia Press, 1978. Offers the definitive biography of John Ross.

Remini, Robert V. *Andrew Jackson: The Course of American Empire, 1767– 1821.* New York: Harper and Row, 1977.

———. *Andrew Jackson: The Course of American Freedom, 1822–1832.* New York: Harper and Row, 1981.

———. *Andrew Jackson: The Course of American Democracy, 1833–1845.* New York: Harper and Row, 1984. Offers together, as three volumes, one of the standard accounts of Andrew Jackson's life.

Ruskin, Gertrude. *Sequoyah, Cherokee Indian Cadmus.* Weaverville, NC: Crowder's Printing Press, 1870. Provides another early account of Sequoyah and the Cherokee literacy revolution.

Schlesinger, Arthur M., Jr. *The Age of Jackson.* Boston: Little, Brown, 1945. Gives an award-winning, if celebratory, look at Andrew Jackson and the idea of "Jacksonianism."

Ward, William. *Andrew Jackson: Symbol for an Age.* New York: Oxford University Press, 1955. Considers Andrew Jackson as a symbol for various movements, reforms, and impulses in the United States.

Wilkins, Thurman. *Cherokee Tragedy: The Story of the Ridge Family and the Decimation of a People.* 2nd ed. Norman: University of Oklahoma Press, 1986. Considers the Trail of Tears and its aftermath specifically from the perspective of the Ridge family; offers the definitive biography of the Ridges.

Slavery Sources

Abel, Annie Heloise. *The American Indian as Slaveholder and Secessionist.* Lincoln: University of Nebraska Press, 1992. Represents the classic work on Native American, including Cherokee, slaveholders.

Davis, J. B. "Slavery in the Cherokee Nation." *Chronicles of Oklahoma* 11 (December 1933): 1056–1072. Investigates the practice of Cherokee slavery.

Halliburton, R. *Red over Black: Black Slavery among the Cherokee Indians.* Westport, CT: Greenwood Press, 1977. Provides an in-depth investigation of the institution of slavery in the Cherokee Nation.

Nash, Gary. *Red, White, and Black: The Peoples of Colonial America*. 3rd ed. Englewood Cliffs, NJ: Prentice Hall, 1992. Explores the interactions and relationships between American Indians, Europeans, and Africans in Colonial America.

Perdue, Theda. *Slavery and the Evolution of Cherokee Society, 1540–1866*. Knoxville: University of Tennessee Press, 1979. Considers slavery's impact on Cherokee society in terms of Cherokee acculturation.

Other Related Sources

Brown, John P. *Old Frontiers: The Story of the Cherokee Indians from Earliest Times to the Date of Their Removal*. Kingsport, TN: Southern Publishers, 1938. Gives an early and sweeping account of the Cherokees through the Trail of Tears.

Champagne, Duane. *Social Order and Political Change: Constitutional Governments among the Cherokee, the Choctaw, the Chickasaw, and the Creek*. Stanford, CA: Stanford University Press, 1992. Explores the Cherokee government as compared to those of other "Civilized Tribes."

Cotterill, R. S. *The Southern Indians: The Story of the Civilized Tribes before Removal*. Norman: University of Oklahoma Press, 1954. Places the Cherokees in their geographic context with other Southern native nations before removal.

Denson, Andrew. *Demanding the Cherokee Nation: Indian Autonomy and American Culture, 1830–1900*. Lincoln: University of Nebraska Press, 2004. Investigates the impulse for Cherokee sovereignty, and the Cherokee use of U.S. founding rhetoric, during and after removal.

Dowd, Gregory Evans. *A Spirited Resistance: The North American Indian Struggle for Unity, 1745–1815*. Baltimore: Johns Hopkins University Press, 1992. Considers Native American opposition to the United States, including the pan-tribal movement led by Tecumseh.

Goodwin, Gary C. *Cherokees in Transition*. Chicago: Department of Geography, University of Chicago, 1977. Examines changes in Cherokee culture and environment prior to the founding of the United States.

Heidler, David S., and Jeanne T. Heidler. *Old Hickory's War: Andrew Jackson and the Quest for Empire*. Mechanicsburg, PA: Stackpole Books, 1996. Investigates Andrew Jackson's actions in the Creek and First Seminole wars.

Foreman, Grant. *The Five Civilized Tribes*. Norman: University of Oklahoma Press, 1932. Represents one of the classic texts on the history of the Cherokee, Choctaw, Chickasaw, Creek, and Seminole nations.

Hatley, M. Thomas. *The Dividing Paths: Cherokees and South Carolinians through the Era of Revolution*. New York: Oxford University Press,

1992. Considers the relationship between the Cherokee Nation and the state of South Carolina during the colonial and revolutionary eras.

Jaimes, H. Annette, ed. *The State of Native America: Genocide, Colonization, and Resistance.* Norman: University of Oklahoma Press, 1988. Provides a collection of essays from various Native American studies perspectives, including international law and demographics.

Jennings, Francis. *The Invasion of America: Indians, Colonialism, and the Cant of Conquest.* Chapel Hill: University of North Carolina Press, 1975. Represents the classic work that challenged the traditional understanding of North America as a "virgin land" prior to European colonization.

King, Duane H., ed. *The Cherokee Indian Nation: A Troubled History.* Knoxville: University of Tennessee Press, 1979. Offers a one-volume history of the Cherokee Nation before, during, and after removal.

Meyers, Marvin. *The Jacksonian Persuasion: Politics and Belief.* Stanford, CA: Stanford University Press, 1960. Considers the politics and ideologies involved with "Jacksonianism."

Perdue, Theda. "Rising from the Ashes: *The Cherokee Phoenix* as an Ethnographical Source." *Ethnohistory* 24, no. 3 (Summer 1977): 207–218. Examines what articles in *The Cherokee Phoenix* reflected about Cherokee culture.

Prucha, Francis Paul. *Great Father: The United States Government and the American Indians.* Lincoln: University of Nebraska Press, 1984. Offers a one-volume history of U.S.–Native American political relations.

Reid, John Phillip. *A Law of Blood: The Primitive Law of the Cherokee Nation.* New York: New York University Press, 1979. Provides a history of the Cherokee legal tradition.

Remini, Robert V. *Andrew Jackson and His Indian Wars.* New York: Viking, 2001. Considers Andrew Jackson's involvement and leadership roles in various "Indian Wars."

Sheehan, Bernard. *Seeds of Extinction: Jeffersonian Philanthropy and the American Indian.* Chapel Hill: University of North Carolina Press, 1973. Examines Thomas Jefferson's personal attitude and political policy toward Native America.

Starkey, Marion L. *The Cherokee Nation.* New York: Knopf, 1946. Offers an older, classic account of Cherokee history before, during, and after removal.

Strickland, Rennard. *Fire and the Spirits: Cherokee Law from Clan to Court.* Norman: University of Oklahoma Press, 1975. Provides a history of Cherokee legal practices and how they changed based on the influence of colonial and U.S. institutions.

Sturgis, Amy H. "Tale of Tears." *Reason* (March 1999): 46–52. Investigates the Bureau of Indian Affairs's occupation of the Cherokee Nation in 1997, and places this event in its historical context.

Thornton, Russell. *American Indian Holocaust and Survival: A Population History since 1492.* Norman: University of Oklahoma Press, 1987. Provides a detailed study of Native American populations, including the loss of life during removal.

———. *The Cherokees: A Population History.* Lincoln: University of Nebraska Press, 1990. Focuses specifically on Cherokee demographics.

Walker, Willard. "The Design of Native Literacy Programs and How Literacy Came to the Cherokees." *Anthropological Linguistics.* 26 (1984): 161–169. Uses an anthropological linguistics approach to consider the Cherokee literacy revolution.

———. "Notes on Native Writing Systems and the Design of Native Literacy Programs." *Anthropological Linguistics* 2 (1969): 151. Considers the Cherokee syllabary in relation to Native American writing systems.

———. "The Roles of Samuel A. Worcester and Elias Boudinot in The Emergence of a Printed Cherokee Syllabic Literature." *International Journal of American Linguistics* 52 (1985): 610–612. Explores Samuel Worcester's and Elias Boudinot's linguistic writings and their effect on Cherokee literature.

Walker, Willard, and James Sarbaugh. "The Early History of the Cherokee Syllabary." *Ethnohistory* 40, no. 1 (Winter 1993): 70–94. Investigates the early story of Sequoyah's Cherokee writing system.

Wardell, Morris. *A Political History of the Cherokee Nation, 1838–1907.* 2nd ed. Norman: University of Oklahoma Press, 1979. Follows the political history of the Cherokees through the removal and post-removal eras.

Woodward, Grace Steele. *The Cherokees.* Norman: University of Oklahoma Press, 1963. Offers a classic one-volume history of the Cherokee Nation.

Young, Mary. "The Cherokee Nation: Mirror of the Republic." *American Quarterly*, no. 33 (Winter 1980): 502–524. Considers Cherokee political acculturation and accommodation in the early U.S. republic.

Websites

The Avalon Project at Yale Law School: Documents in Law, History, and Diplomacy. http://www.yale.edu/lawweb/avalon/avalon.htm. Includes documents relating to U.S. Native American policy.

National Park Service: Trail of Tears. http://www.nps.gov/trte/pphtml/facilities. html. Offers the National Park Service's information on the National Historic Trail.

Teaching with Historic Places Lesson Plans: The Trail of Tears and the Forced Relocation of the Cherokee Nation. http://www.cr.nps.gov/nr/twhp/wwwlps/lessons/118trail/118trail.htm. Provides maps, readings, images, and activities for teaching or learning about the Trail of Tears.

Trail of Tears Association. http://www.nationaltota.org/. Represents the official website of the Trail of Tears Association.

Videotapes and DVDs

"Removal." Episode of *500 Nations*. Warner Home Video, 1995. Investigates the era of Indian removal in general, with specific attention to the Trail of Tears, narrated by Kevin Costner.

"The Trail of Tears." Episode of *How the West Was Lost*. Discovery Enterprises Group, 1993. Focuses primarily on the Cherokee removal experience.

The Trail of Tears. Rich-Heape Films, Inc., 2006. Represents the only Native American–produced documentary about the Cherokee removal experience, hosted in English and Cherokee by Cherokee actor Wes Studi, and narrated by James Earl Jones.

"The Tribes of the Southeast." Episode of *The Native Americans*. TBS Productions, Inc., 1994. Includes interviews with Native American leaders, scholars, and artists, and includes history about the Trail of Tears and contemporary Cherokee culture, as well as additional information on other native nations from the Southeast.

INDEX

About the Author

AMY H. STURGIS is assistant professor of interdisciplinary studies at Belmont University. She is the author of numerous books, book chapters, and articles about Native Americans, science fiction/fantasy, and other topics, including *Presidents from Washington through Monroe, 1789–1825* (Greenwood, 2001) and *Presidents from Hayes through McKinley, 1877–1901* (Greenwood, 2003). Her official website is www.amyhsturgis.com.

Recent Titles in
Greenwood Guides to Historic Events, 1500–1900